The

Volunteer

Recruitment

(And ... ment)

Th...

SUSAN J. ELLIS

Library of Congress Cataloging-in -Publication Data

Ellis, Susan J.
    The volunteer recruitment (and membership development) book / Susan J. Ellis.–3rd ed.
      p. cm.
    Includes bibliographical references and index.
    ISBN 0-940576-25-2
     1. Volunteers–Recruiting. I. Title.

    HN49.V64 E444 2002
    361.3'7'0683–dc21

                                   2001058625

Copyright © 2002 by Energize, Inc.
                    5450 Wissahickon Avenue
                    Philadelphia, PA 19144
                    215-438-8342
                    www.energizeinc.com

ISBN 0-940576-25-2 Third edition.

Third edition, 2002.
Second edition, 1996.
First edition, 1994.

PRINTED IN THE UNITED STATES OF AMERICA

Acknowledgments

Much of the material in this book was developed by "field testing" in real-life situations. The validity of the suggested recruitment techniques has been proven in volunteer projects I have managed myself and in my consultation work with a wide range of different volunteer programs. Thoughts and suggestions from my clients and from participants in my recruitment training workshops over almost twenty years have all found their way into these pages. For all the feedback, innumerable shared ideas, and active questioning, thank you.

In compiling my outline for this book, I pulled together a lot of my previous writing on recruitment. I was surprised to see how much I had written on this subject over the years in workshop handouts, my *NonProfit Times* column, and articles in various publications. The "Proximity Chart" concept first appeared in the original edition of *No Excuses: The Team Approach to Volunteer Management*, which Katie Noyes Campbell and I wrote in 1981. It feels good to have had the chance to rework and update everything, and to have all my thoughts on volunteer recruitment together in one place for the first time.

I owe a great deal of appreciation to the colleagues and friends who reviewed and contributed to various manuscript versions of the book-in-progress: Katie Noyes Campbell, Maggi Davern, Janet Unger, Kristin Floyd, Kris Berggren, Lise Gaulé, and a special thank you to Jeff Kahn for his careful and helpful editing. As always, love to my mother, Ann Ellis, for her proofreading. The attractive look of this book is due to the design expertise of Jonel Sofian. Writing this book was solitary at times, but you all made it feel like a team effort. I'm grateful.

The positive reaction to the first edition of this book has been enormously gratifying. Thanks to all who have given me supportive feedback. For this second edition, special appreciation goes to Cliff Landesman and Bruce Bechtold for their input into the new appendix on cyberspace, Diane Miljat for her bright new cover design, and the crew at Kutztown Publishing for their production help.

A new century and a new edition! It's now 2002 and the Internet has continued to expand in size and importance. So this book needed a new Appendix on cyberspace. This time around I want to thank all the people who have taught me so much about electronic communication in these past years, most notably Kristin Floyd—the best Web Architect ever—and Jayne Cravens—the guru of the Virtual Volunteering Project.

Contents

Introduction

Is recruiting volunteers part of your job? Is this an assignment that you like? Or do you feel dread at the thought of "twisting people's arms" to do you "the favor" of helping your organization?

Like so many other things in life, success as a recruiter of volunteers is highly dependent on attitude. If you can't imagine that anyone will volunteer for you, they probably won't. On the other hand, if you approach recruiting with a positive set of expectations, you will find that people will indeed join up.

Inexperienced volunteer program managers think that recruitment is going to be the hardest thing they do. Here's some good news: recruiting volunteers is generally not hard. People will come forward and offer their help if you actively spread the word about your organization's needs. The actual problem is something altogether different:

Having meaningful work for people to do once they've joined up!

After all, the best recruiter in the world will soon get burned out if a revolving door has new recruits enter, become disillusioned, and then leave. For this reason, we will focus carefully in the first few chapters on designing volunteer work. If you are constantly recruiting new people because current volunteers are departing, *stop* recruiting until you have analyzed *why* retention is a problem.

Another thing that may be difficult is:

Eliciting applications from the most qualified prospective volunteers.

Your goal as a recruiter is not to elicit hundreds of inquiries from folks with unknown and unproven skills. Instead, the most successful volunteer recruiters are those who can *focus* so specifically on vacant assignments that only qualified candidates come forward. If one prospective volunteer applies, but that person suits the position to a tee, then you've done your recruiting job splendidly.

The inexperienced recruiter prints 5,000 brochures and then muses: "where can I distribute these?" The experienced—and more effective—recruiter *first* asks: "where might I find the right volunteers for each job?"—and then selects the best technique to match each potential source. So this book will guide you through the process of targeted "mini-campaigns," always organized around the best places to look for volunteers, rather than on "how" to get a message across. Blanketing your community with recruitment messages is rarely time- or cost-effective.

It is possible that you have been generally successful at recruiting volunteers for most available assignments but that you have found certain positions extremely difficult to fill. Or, your recruitment obstacle may be an inability to attract a particular type of volunteer, or someone in another geographic area, or some other needed variable. Clearly some volunteer roles are more attractive than others and you may have to expend more energy on those that seem less desirable. But the suggestions in this book should help you to refine both what you are asking volunteers to do and where you look to recruit prospective candidates.

1

Finally, another possible challenge is:

The world is changing and volunteerism is changing with it.

This truism is only a "problem" if you want to fight the tide. In the recent past, many agency volunteer programs relied on just a few sources of volunteers. If your organization's volunteer force has been mainly "traditional," you may well hear others tell you that "volunteering is dying out." Well I, for one, cannot bemoan the women's movement nor many of the other trends that have shaken the paid and unpaid workforce. Chapter 5 will look at these and other issues more closely. The bottom line is that many volunteers are still available to those organizations willing to adapt and diversify. How aware is your organization of social changes and does your recruitment reflect this?

Much of the material in this book is relevant to any *marketing* challenge. You may, in fact, find it useful to do some reading of business-oriented marketing textbooks to supplement some of the points raised here. Do not be turned off by the concept of "marketing." It is not out of place in the nonprofit or government environment. Classically, marketing is the process of understanding your customers, developing products they want and need, and finding the ways to tell them about the opportunity to do business with you. Is this not one way of describing volunteer recruitment? I'll use volunteer-related vocabulary more familiar to you, but occasionally I will refer to marketing concepts.

It is probably worthwhile to note that the term recruitment is used for searches other than for volunteers. Some of you will be in organizations recruiting people who can use your services: a literacy program may be looking for reading students or a women's health center may want to attract pregnant teenagers. The tips on volunteer recruitment here work for any type of recruitment—including finding good employees!

This book will examine the tasks of recruitment in depth. But recruitment does not exist in a vacuum. If you are unfamiliar with the skills of developing and running a volunteer effort, you will need to add other knowledge to your repertoire. For example, how to prepare your organization for volunteer involvement, how to develop teamwork between volunteers and employees, orientation and training for volunteers, techniques of volunteer supervision, recordkeeping and reporting, evaluation, recognition—all of these must be in place or your recruitment will be hollow. In fact, word will spread rapidly if you put out a call for volunteers before you are ready! Ultimately, the best recruitment strategy is to make sure that each and every volunteer has **a great experience** with your organization. That will make future recruitment much easier.

Volunteer recruitment is one element in a broader picture of how your organization wants to function in the community. In a very real sense, the involvement of volunteers is a form of *resource development* and, as a recruiter, you are engaged in "people raising" just as a development officer is engaged in fund raising. I therefore believe that a leader of volunteers has a double mandate:

1. To identify the needs of the organization's clients/public and paid staff; and, then

2. To *mobilize noncash resources in the community* to meet those needs.

This is a strong and ambitious vision for the role of volunteer manager and for the goals of volunteer recruitment. Note that this approach is based on meeting needs in noncash ways, which opens the door to a wide variety of assistance regardless of whether it is labelled "volunteer." Most of the time, you will be mobilizing noncash, *human* resources, but in-kind services and donated items may also fill a critical need. I hope that this book will broaden your horizons about the range of potential resources and about you as *catalyst*.

The variety of organizations seeking volunteers is enormous and so each reader will have different needs and concerns. However, I strongly feel that the basic concepts in this book are equally relevant to large and small agencies, urban and rural settings, and to any field of endeavor. The similarities simply outweigh the differences when it comes to the principles of why people volunteer. However, when there are some pointers more relevant to an urban or to a rural setting, I have tried to address them throughout the chapters.

As with any book for a broad audience, I have tried to present the most common scenarios shared by the majority of settings involving volunteers. This means that I have assumed you are either with an agency wishing to integrate volunteers with the work of a paid staff or that you are with a pre-dominantly all-volunteer organization. But some of you may be on the edges of the bell-shaped curve. For example, if you need three hundred volunteers for a two-day event such as a golf tournament, the suggestions here should help you but will need special adaptation. Similarly, if all of your volunteers come from within a pre-established set of client participants, as in a senior center, you will also have to pick and choose the pointers most relevant to you.

An ethical principle: This book is not designed to help one organization be better at recruiting than another. In an ideal world, all worthy organizations would have all the volunteers they need. The point is not to convince prospective volunteers that the deaf need more help than the blind. *All* your causes and clients deserve attention. Rather, the goal of a recruiter is to show individuals where *they* might *best contribute their special talents*.

If you are an officer of an all-volunteer organization and are hoping that this book will help you with "membership development," take heart. I will do my best to say "volunteers and members" whenever possible, but do not let vocabulary put you off. All of the concepts of volunteer recruitment are meaningful for all-volunteer efforts who want to expand their membership rolls . . . and who want to transform "members" into active *workers*. Even though all of Chapter 13 is written specifically for you, I recommend that you work your way through the chapters that precede it, to set the context. (I also hope that agency-related readers will not skip Chapter 13! Many of the ideas there are relevant to working with volunteers in any group, including auxiliaries or special committees.)

The point of view of *The Volunteer Recruitment Book* is that of one organization seeking volunteers. But you may be with a Volunteer Center, RSVP, student community service office, or other program with the mission of recruiting many volunteers and then referring or placing them into a variety of sites in the community. You may also be working at the national level of an organization with state or other local affiliates—all of whom want to find more volunteers. In your situation, you have the challenge of "paving the way" for your constituents, making sure that a large number of people learn and get excited about the potential of volunteering. You work on behalf of all the placement sites you represent, but you are once removed from the actual things volunteers will do. I think that much of the material in this book will be helpful to you, though some things such as job design may be out of your control. Of course, you can really help your placement sites if you assist them to be *ready* for the volunteers you will find together. In the last analysis, however, the greatest support you can give is to raise the public's *awareness* of volunteering. By the way, you will find yourself referred to in this book as both a *source* of volunteers and a *technique* of recruitment for individual agencies! It's all a matter of perspective.

In the last analysis, the only way to get volunteers is to **ask people to volunteer!** As we are about to discuss, it is easy to confuse publicity or public relations with volunteer recruitment. Until you are actively asking people to help, you cannot evaluate the results of your recruitment efforts. Also, while one-to-one recruitment of new volunteers by current volunteers is an excellent way to identify new people, you cannot rely on such word of mouth alone to bring in new volunteers with diverse skills, of both sexes, or of different ethnic groups. You must purposely seek out such candidates and tell them that you want their involvement.

The chapters that follow will guide you, step by step, to a successful recruitment effort. I guarantee it. I cannot promise that you will fill every position nor that all the volunteers you will find will have the perfect schedules or the perfect credentials. But the techniques described here do work. They are logical and welcoming. Best of all, you will find them manageable . . . maybe even fun. (And here's a secret: if you enjoy recruiting volunteers, you'll be better at it!)

Recruitment Is the Third Step

It is common for veterans in the volunteer management field to be approached by newcomers with worries about being able to find volunteers. "Please give me hints about how to recruit" is the plea. The proper response is: "First tell me what you want volunteers to *do*."

Recruitment of volunteers is only one step in a process that begins with thoughtful planning and ends with genuine teamwork of everyone, paid or not, working toward common goals. When done at the right time and in the right way, recruitment will produce results. But all too often organizations jump the gun, spreading word of their hope for volunteer help prematurely. And then the trouble starts. Without the preparation we are about to discuss in the next few chapters, you run the risk of bringing out people who do not really meet your needs and therefore are the wrong volunteers for you. And having the wrong volunteers may be worse than having no volunteers at all.

Here is an overview of the basic steps of recruitment which we will then cover in greater detail in the following chapters.

The First Step: Know Why Your Organization Wants Volunteers

This is not a foolish question and the answer is often not self-evident. Too many people assume that the major reason organizations recruit volunteers is that there is not enough money to do the necessary work and so volunteers are the next best thing. As I have discussed at length in *From the Top Down: The Executive Role in Volunteer Program Success* (Energize, 1986), this is a negative perception. It makes volunteers a "second choice." The corollary would be: "If we had enough money, we wouldn't need (or even want) volunteers."

An organization that has not articulated why it wants volunteers in the first place may find recruiting difficult. Whether intentional or not, people may hear the message: "we don't necessarily want volunteers, but since we don't have more money, would you do us a favor and help out?" Hardly a motivating sales pitch!

Conversely, if an organization values volunteers for the *unique* benefits they bring, the recruitment message changes considerably. For example: "We welcome volunteers because your support shows that the community really wants this organization to succeed." Or, "volunteers diversify and expand the skills we can offer to our consumers." Or, "it really matters to our clients that volunteers want to help; they sometimes feel that staff members only help because it's their job." Such "first choice" reasons for involving volunteers show everyone that money plus trained employees plus concerned volunteers *together* equal the best service to consumers.

The issue of limited money is valid, of course, but only as one factor. Never say or imply that volunteers "save" money because that is not true. Instead, consider such descriptions as: "Involving volunteers allows us to *stretch the budget* way beyond what we otherwise might be able to afford," or "volunteers let us spend every dollar we have

5

and then *do more.*" Such statements are motivating to prospective volunteers as well as being accurate.

I am recommending that you take the time to articulate your organization's reasons for involving volunteers, write these down, and make sure everyone agrees. This gives you a foundation on which to define the work volunteers will do, to create better teamwork between employees and volunteers, and —the key point for us here—to use this statement of purpose in your recruiting presentations.

Once you have articulated why your organization wants volunteers at all, the next challenge is to determine what volunteers are expected to *accomplish.* After all, having volunteers is not an end unto itself. Volunteers are a *resource* and a *strategy* for fulfilling the organization's mission. Set specific goals and objectives for volunteer achievement—and I don't mean just numerical quotas for how many volunteers you want. How will volunteers make a difference in service delivery?

On an annual basis, evaluate whether volunteers have indeed accomplished something meaningful. Review and revise the goals and objectives for volunteer participation. Then use these to show prospective recruits how their efforts will make a difference in your organization's work.

The Second Step: Design Valuable Volunteer Assignments

This step is truly crucial to providing service to your organization and to being successful in recruitment. You want to design volunteer assignments that accomplish real work and that are attractive to prospective volunteers.

I cannot stress this point enough. If the only work you ask volunteers to do is low-level and unchallenging, you will generally only recruit people who prefer that type of assignment. If you design volunteer roles that are demanding, creative, or sophisticated, you will *attract* volunteers who are interested in that type of work. Isn't the same thing true for employee jobs?

"Challenging" and "creative" are subjective terms, of course. Just because you personally do not find a task interesting does not mean that someone else will not be fascinated by it. The point, however, is to raise your organization's vision about the potential of what volunteers can do. Limited vision produces limited results. You may need volunteers to do very basic tasks, but these should be valuable and valued—and may only be the start of how volunteers can contribute.

Some people subscribe to the theory that first you should spread the word of your need for volunteers and then create volunteer assignments to suit the candidates who come in. This is definitely not my approach, although I hope you will be creative in reacting to unexpected talents that are offered to you (we'll come back to this in later chapters). As a basic strategy, however, I believe that you begin by knowing your need for help and then do your recruiting to assure that you will find it. This is a proactive, not reactive, process.

Because the need to define volunteer work is so important, we will devote all of Chapter 2 to this subject. Chapter 3 examines the question of why people volunteer and why others do not—a subject that closely connects with job design. The more you know about the motivation of volunteers, the more you can refine your volunteer job descriptions to be appealing.

The Third Step: Develop and Implement Your Recruitment Plan

I don't want to keep you in suspense. Right here and now let me outline the tasks necessary for successful recruitment of volunteers:

Task A. For *each* volunteer job description, **brainstorm potential *sources*** of people having the necessary qualifications. (Then edit the list of ideas to include variables such as feasibility, cost, and possible diversity of candidates.)

Task B. For *each* potential source of volunteers, **select the most appropriate technique** to communicate your message. (You wouldn't give a speech with slides at an all-night laundromat.)

Task C. **Do it!** Go out and *ask* people to volunteer.

Task D. **Be prepared** for applicants to contact you and develop a welcoming system for interviewing, screening, and putting new volunteers to work.

As you become successful in recruiting volunteers, focus your attention on the most important step of all:

Keep volunteers motivated with training, ongoing communication, supervision, evaluation, and recognition.

After all, if your volunteer corps unexpectedly turns over every six months, your recruitment efforts have been wasted. And ultimately your goal is to have a self-perpetuating cycle in which satisfied volunteers bring in more volunteers.

Chapter 6 and all of Section II describe each of the recruiting tasks in depth.

The Logic of this Recruitment Strategy

As I hope to prove in the chapters to come, there is an elegant logic to following the steps as outlined above and in the sequence presented. I am recommending that you never conduct a community-wide, cast-the-net, general, "we need volunteers" recruitment campaign. Instead, I strongly urge you to do a series of "mini-campaigns" focused on *each volunteer assignment* or on whatever special needs you have. The more you *focus*, the greater your chances for success and (wonder of wonders!) the less work you will create for yourself as a recruiter.

Recruitment is both a *process* and an *activity*. Although we use the word "recruitment" for both, it is helpful to see the distinction. As a process, recruitment involves all the preparation and follow-through necessary to create a welcoming environment for volunteers. The process must involve your whole organization, because volunteers must mesh with the work done by everyone. As an activity, recruitment is the task of *asking*, of

inviting individuals and groups to become volunteers.

When you bought this book, you might have started with questions about the *activity* of recruiting: "how do I do it?" It is my hope that by the time you are done reading, you will be so comfortable with the *process* of recruitment that the ways you communicate with the public will be a natural extension of your vision of volunteer involvement.

The Context for Recruitment

In order to meet your recruitment goals, you also have to broaden your thinking past the specific needs of the moment. The more informed you are about the *context* of your recruitment challenge, the better able you will be to design your search effectively. So in addition to the steps just outlined, you also need to:

1. Analyze the image of your organization in the community.

2. Examine the other related images that affect volunteer recruitment.

3. Consider the trends and issues in the field of volunteerism today.

Because these three areas are of major significance in the recruitment process, we will deal with them at length in Chapters 4 and 5. You will see that they are absolutely necessary before "going public" with any invitation to volunteer. The good news is that all of the analysis and thinking recommended in these chapters will be done for your volunteer needs *as a whole*. So, once you have completed the diagnoses and decision-making, you should not have to do it again, except to keep it updated.

Membership Development

All of the techniques discussed in this book are adaptable to all-volunteer membership organizations. But there are some special issues when your challenge is encouraging people to "join" a group or motivating inactive members to participate more. Chapter 13 will focus on those concerns.

SECTION I:

PREPARATION

The chapters in Section I discuss all of the things you need to do before actually asking anyone to volunteer. These are the steps to take to plan for volunteer involvement and to select the best sources of prospective volunteers for your available assignments.

A Fresh Look at Volunteer Job Design

Defining the work that volunteers will do is the foundation for all of your recruitment efforts. After all, if there were no tasks for volunteers to complete, you wouldn't be bothering to invite people to volunteer! Volunteers are a resource for accomplishing real work.

As I have already said, the types of volunteer roles you design have a direct correlation to whom you can attract to fill those roles. The more creative, sophisticated, skilled, or fun the things you ask volunteers to do, the more you can expect to find volunteers who match (keeping in mind that such adjectives are subjective and that what turns one person off may turn another on). If, after following some of the suggestions in this chapter, you still end up with limited volunteer roles, your best recruitment strategy might be to find volunteers for whom even these roles are a challenge: preteens, participants in a sheltered workshop program, or people seeking beginner-level skills for a short time. The point is to avoid inviting skillful people to become volunteers and then to underutilize them (what a waste!).

You may well be recruiting for a cause or agency that evokes deep loyalty. People who "burn" to be involved will gladly do even "menial" labor. This is neither wrong nor evil—and much necessary work gets done because of this type of strong commitment. For example, why would such a wide range of people be willing to clean up vacant lots or glean fruit fields? However, just because some individuals will do "anything" to help, is not enough justification to be uncreative in putting their talents to good use!

Let's look at some options for identifying your organization's needs and deciding how volunteers might meet those needs. But please note that subsequent chapters will raise issues that may send you "back to the drawing board" to refine or adapt your initial job descriptions. It may take some experimentation to find the right mix of challenge and ease, work and play, formality and informality in your set of volunteer positions. There are very few rules about what you might ask volunteers to do. So be inventive!

Task Analysis

Volunteer job design is a challenge of "task analysis," since almost by definition volunteer work is done in limited chunks of time. Your responsibility is to examine the many services your organization provides and carve out meaningful assignments that can be accomplished in two to four hour intervals, perhaps weekly or even periodically. It is not enough to say "we need volunteer help." You are aiming to develop a series of quite specific jobs for which you can recruit different types of volunteers.

Avoid asking the *wrong* question, which is: "What can volunteers do to help us?" The answers you will hear to this query will be based on stereotypes about volunteers. For example, if someone thinks most volunteers are pleasant but largely unskilled amateurs, what type of work will s/he identify for such low-level helpers to do?

The *right* question is: "What needs to be done

around here?'' Begin by identifying *all* of the unmet needs of clients and staff. List both large and small projects, including the things that have been on people's "wish lists" for a long time. You are not promising that volunteers can be found to do all of these things, but you have to know what work is required or desired before you can develop a strategy for recruiting the types of volunteers able to handle those tasks.

To get the creative juices flowing, ask some thought-provoking questions such as:

- What are we doing now that we would like to do *more* of?
- What *unmet needs* do our clients/consumers have that we presently can do nothing about?
- What would *support* the staff in their work?
- What might we do *differently* if we had more skills or time available to us?

Another way to expand people's thinking is to ask: "How would we spend an unexpected windfall of $250,000 (or some other outrageous sum), if we had to use it all in one year?" This leads people to think about all the things they wish they could do but never expect the resources with which to do it. It elicits discussion of whole new service arenas, not just what would "assist" present staff. These are the type of dreams from which volunteer projects might be created.

Who Designs the Work

The leader of volunteers cannot and should not develop volunteer assignments alone. This responsibility is shared with everyone in the organization, particularly with those staff members who will ultimately work side-by-side with volunteers to get the work done. Creating volunteer roles is the start of the entire process of welcoming and integrating volunteers into the organization.

There can be conflict between what volunteers want to do and how organizations create volunteer projects. Because many paid workers are overworked and have little time to devote to thinking about volunteers, volunteer assignments are too often created quickly and without much respect for the skills or interests of those who will fill them. In fairness, it is difficult to parcel out

work when volunteer time is provided in short fragments, but the real problem is usually shaky faith in the abilities of volunteers. It therefore seems less risky to limit volunteers to tangential, icing-on-the-cake roles that are "nice" but would not be missed if the volunteer proves undependable.

But for the volunteer, the time carved out of a busy schedule for volunteer work is quite precious. Volunteers hope that their contributed time will have real meaning, have an impact or make a difference. Given the choice, people would select the volunteer assignment that accomplishes the most—in fact, that is the whole point. And ethically, volunteers trust organizations not to put them to work doing unproductive activity.

So, for you as the coordinator of volunteers, helping paid staff to design the most meaningful work for volunteers is the way to begin training employees about the potential of community participation.

Volunteer Job Design Considerations

There are many ways to approach the development of volunteer assignments. Your goal is to have as diverse a set of volunteer job descriptions as possible, which will help you when you are ready to recruit. Think about:

- Both continuous, ongoing volunteer assignments, and also short-term and one-time work projects.
- Things individual volunteers can do, and also what teams of two or three volunteers, or larger groups of people, can do. This may include families volunteering as a unit or such concepts as "job sharing."
- Periodic assignments that allow the volunteer to be "on call" to help as necessary.
- Work that can be done by anyone willing to be taught what to do ("generalist" positions) versus work that requires volunteers already having proven skills ("specialist" positions).
- Work that can be done on-site or off-site.
- Assignments dealing with people, with

things, or with ideas.
- Hands-on work, or thinking/planning work, or work based on observation.

For each volunteer assignment you define, be sure to consider how many hours of service will be needed and what schedule would be ideal. For example, are there certain days or times that are priorities for coverage?

Ivan Scheier has dealt at length with the issue of job design in his book, *Building Staff/Volunteer Relations* (Energize, 1993). He proposes such techniques as "job factoring" and the "window of work" to help both paid staff and volunteers discover the best ways that volunteers can participate in achieving service goals. He allows both partners to consider the things they like to do, don't like to do, and wish they could learn to do—all potential elements in a volunteer job description.

As a rule, volunteer assignments are patterned on the job descriptions and schedules of paid staff. This is because volunteers are seen as helpers or assistants to employees. While there is nothing wrong with this frame of reference, it is also limiting. Why not try a more creative approach to designing ways volunteers can contribute?

Keep in mind that volunteers might be flexible with their schedules. It is safe to assume that many of the individual or community needs your organization is addressing exist around the clock. So focus on these needs without defining the "solution" within the confines of a Monday to Friday, 9 to 5 parameter. Here are a few examples of actual volunteer roles that highlight what can be done at unusual hours:

— *A family counseling agency recruited volunteers to telephone assigned families at 7:00 a.m. on school days to provide structure and offer friendly support as parents were preparing their children for school.*

—*A hospital was able to provide additional night services, including a crisis hot line, by recruiting a corps of insomniac volunteers referred by their psychologists (a win-win situation!).*

—*A national labor union involved its members in a project studying how blue collar workers are portrayed on television by ask-*ing for volunteers to watch and report on shows aired throughout a particular period.*

—*A park started a weekend campground patrol program by recruiting families to volunteer at specific camp sites for 48-hour shifts. The multi-generational volunteers proved to be effective role models for the weekend campers.*

There are other criteria that can be used to design creative volunteer roles, especially if you free yourself from the model of what the paid staff does. Consider these examples—again, all are real:

—*A juvenile detention center recruited physically disabled volunteers because it found that people in wheelchairs were particularly effective in confronting teenage lawbreakers about making choices in more positive ways.*

—*A nursing home opened an after-school homework center for latchkey children at a nearby elementary school. It was hard to determine which age group was the most "served" by the interaction.*

—*A hospital created a set of videotapes of young volunteers talking about their own hospital experiences, to be shown by close-circuit television to other child patients receiving similar treatment.*

—*A municipal streets department recruited volunteer block representatives to act as communication liaisons whenever roadwork was going to create temporary detours or other inconveniences.*

—*A professional association offered members the chance to barter special skills for reduced registration at their annual conference. The biggest hit was the member who volunteered to give neck and shoulder massages in the conference headquarters room to frazzled committee members.*

What do all of these examples have in common? They demonstrate how volunteers can meet special needs—often quite targeted needs requiring very part-time or even "off-time" availability.

In most cases, these are tasks that would never become full-time jobs. And in some cases, they would never be budgeted for despite how much they add to the success of a venture.

In addition, these volunteer job descriptions make use of the unique talents or traits of the people contributing their time. No matter how expert employees may be, they still have a finite set of skills. Employees also tend to be homogeneous in terms of educational background and age range. Volunteers therefore diversify what the paid staff can offer to the recipients of service. Make sure that volunteer assignments make use of younger and older people, distinct life experiences, different occupational skills, different languages, and new perspectives.

Finally, make use of the gift of volunteers to focus on one thing at a time. Employees must divide their attention among a full client case load or among everyone requesting service. Volunteers, however, can be recruited specifically to spend all their hours on one child, one research project, one specialized task. This is a luxury with benefits to everyone.

When you let your creative juices flow beyond "staff assistant," you'll see the limitless possibilities for involving volunteers in meaningful work.

Options and Variety

The more ways you develop for people to become involved as volunteers, the easier your recruitment task. Most people prefer to ease into a new situation. So if the only jobs you have available require an initial commitment of two years, expect some resistance. But if you have some volunteer assignments that can be accomplished in a short-term timeframe or even some one-day projects, people can "get their feet wet" before taking the full plunge. By the way, such options also allow *you* to see candidates in action and to assess their work before signing them up for more intensive involvement.

On the other hand, do not be apologetic about the fact that some assignments will indeed require a long-term commitment. Some prospective volunteers will welcome the challenge of a more intensive role.

Rural or small organizations sometimes resist the idea of separating out different volunteer assignments when the total number of volunteers will be small. Their approach is to treat most volunteers as "floaters," doing whatever needs to be done on any given day. There is nothing wrong with the practicality of this approach, but it does tend to homogenize all volunteers. Individual talents are not discussed—and therefore not tapped—because the work is designed for the lowest common denominator (so that anyone can do it). Or, the more skilled volunteers accrue additional tasks without acknowledgment. Analyze what volunteers are really doing for you now. You may be surprised to discover that, even with a small number of volunteers, you already have some variety in job descriptions.

If you do have a small number of volunteers, try developing a "core" volunteer role shared by everyone, accompanied by a set of special tasks focused on unique skills. Then recruit for those, as well. For example, all volunteers could be asked to start each shift by freshening patients' water pitchers, delivering mail or messages, and checking with the nursing station to see who needs some special attention. But once a week, one designated volunteer might also staff the library room, while another volunteer reports to the accounting office to enter data on the computer.

The above idea is also one approach to getting basic tasks done without having to make only one volunteer do them as his or her main job. Divide up the less-appealing tasks among everyone as a small piece of more challenging assignments. This may be a solution to those assignments that seem the hardest to fill: distribute elements of the work so that burdens are shared and let volunteers work in teams to get everything done.

Creating Assignments to Tap Special Help

While most of the time you will initiate the recruitment process by defining priority work to be done and asking people to do it, you may also learn about a possible source of help and want to make use of it. A good example is the "Day of Caring" project or "Making a Difference" event sponsored by a growing number of local United

Ways (often through the Volunteer Center, see page 56). The model here is that volunteers are centrally recruited in groups from corporations and civic organizations to be "deployed" throughout the community for a one-day, intensive burst of help to many different agencies.

If such a resource was available to you, could your organization make use of it? What could twenty strangers do of real help for six hours? This chance to tap group effort might come from any number of sources. What if the group was a class of sixth graders? How about a retired secretaries club?

Go back to your various wish lists and see what projects could be moved forward by a quick "in and out" spurt of service. Some possibilities to consider are:

- Here is where manual labor makes sense. It requires minimal training. It can be shared and made social. So all those clean-up, painting, and fix-up projects are ideal.
- Blanketing a neighborhood with a door-to-door effort of some sort (such as distributing educational literature) maximizes the support and safety of doing such outreach with a lot of people.
- Giving a party or some special program for your clients or public.
- Reorganizing your files, storage room, library— whatever could use many hands so that the disruption and disarray ends as soon as possible.

One-day group projects need not be as formal nor as structured as ongoing assignments, but they do need to be *organized*! The worst thing you can do is to waste the time of any volunteer, even for one day. For this reason, if you really cannot support the group activity well, it is better to say no to the offer of help. Remember, as we said above, a good one-time project can introduce prospective longer-term volunteers to your organization. So this whole idea is really a recruitment technique, as well.

Assessing the Appeal

As you develop your set of volunteer job descriptions, consider the type of person to whom such assignments might appeal. Are you making every assignment an "assistant" or "aide" or are some leadership roles available? Do you expect a lot of physical activity or mostly desk work? How much modern technological knowledge (such as working with computers) is needed? The presence or absence of such elements determines the type of people who might be interested in filling the job.

If you want to recruit a diverse volunteer corps, try to modify the job descriptions to add elements that might appeal to the groups you hope to attract: young men? retired executives? up and coming female managers? new Americans?

Keep in mind that some volunteers may not want direct client or public contact, while others might want this above all else. Some people love variety each time they come in to volunteer, some prefer consistency of tasks.

What Benefits Do You Offer?

In the next chapter we will discuss why people volunteer. The potential motivations are endless. As prospects consider your volunteer openings, they will want to know what you are offering them in exchange for their time. Some of the benefits will be tangible, such as reimbursement for out-of-pocket expenses or certificates for completion of a training program. But the intangibles are important, too. It is up to you to explain what a volunteer can expect to receive. Some possibilities are:

- A new understanding of your cause, client group, or issue.
- Training in a specific skill.
- The opportunity to interact with many different people (or, conversely, with a special type of person).
- The pleasure of being part of a team.
- Insight into one's own abilities and beliefs.
- New friends.
- Something to put on a résumé.
- Feedback on their work.

As you develop jobs for volunteers, articulate

what the benefits are for each assignment. That way, if a graduate student wants to learn about your agency's intake system while a recently-divorced volunteer wants to make new friends, you can match them to the assignments that best meet their interests as well as yours.

Writing Volunteer Job Descriptions

Because the volunteer job itself is the basis for recruiting the most qualified volunteer, it is very important to put it *in writing*. Some people resist the idea of having written volunteer job descriptions because this sounds so bureaucratic or because they are afraid a job description will scare prospective volunteers away. It also takes time to develop good descriptions and to keep them current. Here are a few reasons the effort is worthwhile:

- The *process* of writing each volunteer job description makes everyone think about the work to be done. Is this really a job with enough to do? Is this too much work for one assignment? What training and supervision will the volunteer need and is the staff member or committee chair prepared to provide this?

- Having to create a job description forces staff to think a request through more carefully than a simple "we need help with donated items" (implying, "please take one of your waiting volunteers out of the freezer and send the warmed up body to me"). Instead, articulating the need for a volunteer to record donated items, examine their condition, and sort/store them properly, helps everyone to identify the best type of person for the job (and makes it clear that you will require time to find him or her).

- A written volunteer job description makes sure you (or whoever conducts screening interviews) will discuss the work to be done completely and consistently with each candidate. When shared with applicants, the job description allows prospective volunteers to "self screen" their willingness and/or ability to do the work.

- The job description becomes the basis of ongoing supervision and evaluation of the volunteer—is he or she doing what was agreed to at the start? You can thank volunteers for accomplishing the tasks outlined in their job description. You can also use the written description to compare unsatisfactory work with what was expected.

If you are uncomfortable with the terminology of a "job" description for a volunteer, you can name the form anything you like: "Volunteer Position Description," "Assignment Summary," or any other descriptive phrase. Just be sure you put what you expect volunteers to do in writing.

Elements of a Volunteer Job Description

On the next page is a worksheet for developing a written volunteer job description.

First, make sure every volunteer job is given a *title*. The word "volunteer" is a pay category, not a title! If the work to be done requires a "tutor," "tour guide," or "picnic coordinator," assign a title that reflects the content of the assignment. If the volunteer is going to be in charge of something, let the title show that, too.

The title you select can be intriguing or fun, and therefore of help in recruiting. For example, Ellie Fusaro at the Mt. Vernon Center for Community Mental Health in Virginia sought a volunteer to help maintain her volunteer records. She put out a call for a "Statistical Detective" and quickly found a volunteer eager to meet the challenge!

Next, outline the *responsibilities* of the assignment. Describe sample tasks. Your goal is to define both the potential and the limits of the job, and to make it clear to the reader what will be expected. A section on *outcomes* or *goals* identifies how you and the volunteer will know when the job is being done successfully or when the desired results have been achieved.

Include a description of the *training* and *supervision* the volunteer will receive. How will the person be prepared to do the work well and be supported in doing so?

Be clear on the *timeframe* you need. What are

Volunteer Job Description Worksheet

Position Title: _____
(Remember the word "volunteer" is a pay category, not a title!)

Description of Project/Purpose of Assignment:

Outline of Volunteer's Responsibilities or List of Tasks:
(Give potential and limits.)

Outcomes/Goals:
How will you and the volunteer know that the job is being done well or that the project is successful?

Training and Support Plan:
How will the volunteer be prepared for the work and oriented to the agency? ■ Who will supervise/ be the contact point?

Reporting:
What reports will be expected, in what form and how often?

Time Commitment:
Minimum hours per week/month? On any special schedule? For what duration of time?

Qualifications Needed:

Benefits:
What will the volunteer get in exchange for service (tangibles and intangibles)?

the minimum number of hours necessary per week or month to accomplish the task? Do these have to be offered on any special schedule? For what duration of time will the assignment continue? If the work is ongoing, what is the minimum initial commitment you can accept?

Do not be afraid of stating your needs definitively. It is better to have prospective volunteers know in advance what is truly needed to do the job well, rather than hoping to persuade them later to do more. With an honest job description, when volunteers commit to an assignment, you will know that they are agreeing to do what you have requested. If they cannot fulfill your requirements, isn't it better to know that in advance, instead of discovering it once it is too late? If a volunteer cannot do what is necessary to be the best at a particular assignment, you can always discuss another option with him or her.

The volunteer job description should include a section on what *progress reports* will be expected, in what form, and how often. For some assignments, particularly for volunteers who will be doing most of their work off-site, this is a critical point that deserves clarification from the start.

Finally, include a description of the *qualifications* needed to do the assignment, both in terms of skills and past experience and of personality traits. It is also very worthwhile to have a section on *benefits* to the volunteer. What tangible benefits do you offer, such as transportation expense reimbursement, and what less tangible benefits will be derived, such as career exploration?

Keep volunteer job descriptions updated so that they accurately reflect the work volunteers do for your organization.

Instruction Sheets

It has been my experience that organizations intermingle job descriptions with what are really instruction sheets. This happens most when a volunteer job is very definite and concrete, and will be filled by several people who all have to operate in a consistent way. Examples are receptionist positions, meal preparation assistants, and sports equipment coordinators. In writing the "job description," it is easy to begin listing very specific "do things this way" items, but the instructions

for a job should be clearly separated from the description of the role.

The Sports Equipment Coordinator's job description might list as one area of responsibility: "Will make sure that all equipment distributed during the practice session is returned and properly stored." This is an ongoing *function* of the position. But, details such as, "place football equipment in the cabinet on the left and soccer equipment on the shelves in the basement" are *current procedures* that may change over time.

Because procedural instructions are indeed important to explain, especially if any are legal regulations or vital safety rules, you actually draw more attention to them by making a *separate* page entitled something like "Work Guidelines" or "To-Do List." The cover sheet is the volunteer job description outlining the purpose and context of the assignment and the attached sheets give the instructions.

For a one-time special event, you may find that what you need more than a complete job description is excellent instruction sheets—even check lists. Develop an instruction sheet for each volunteer assignment area (you might even use color coding to make it easy to tell one from the other). At the top, start with a paragraph explaining the general goals of the assignment and how it fits with the other work being done that day by other volunteers and employees. Then list the instructions and rules. End the sheet with a clearly-marked box telling what to do and whom to ask (and where to find that person) if something unexpected arises!

Group Work Descriptions

Job descriptions are as important for group volunteering as for individual volunteer roles. First you need a "Project Description" defining the main elements of the work to be done (see page 19). Include such things as:

- Goals for the project.
- What the lines of communication will be between your organization and the group (who is responsible for each side).
- The number of participants and/or hours of coverage needed to make the project happen.

Group Volunteer Project Description Worksheet

Project: _____

Date(s) work is to be done: _____

Description of Project:

Outline of Major Responsibilities or List of Tasks:
(Summarize here. Then attach individual job descriptions or instruction sheets.)

Number of volunteers needed to complete the work:
(Or number of hours of coverage needed)

Qualifications Needed:

Outcomes/Goals:
How will you and the group know that the job is being done well or that the project is successful?

Training and Support Plan:
How will everyone be prepared for the work and oriented to the agency? ■ Who will supervise/be the contact point in your organization? ■ Who will supervise/be the contact point in the organization that accepts this group assignment?

Reporting:
What reports will be expected, in what form and how often?

Benefits:
What will the group (and individual volunteers) get in exchange for service (tangibles and intangibles)?

- A list of the specific tasks needed to be covered.
- Orientation and training plan.
- Reporting plan.

If a group is taking responsibility for a complete project, you may need to create a set of individual job descriptions to accompany the Project Description. You will almost certainly at a minimum need some instruction sheets. The group leader can then recruit/designate specific members to fulfill each assignment.

The Characteristics You Are Seeking

Now that you have done all of this, there is one more task you need to do: define the "ideal profile" of a volunteer in each job description. These are the characteristics that you hope you will find in those who apply to be volunteers.

Are you hoping that volunteers in a particular assignment will be in a certain age range? Do you want a variety of races and ethnic groups? Is there a personality type that is best suited to this role? We are not talking about discrimination, but affirmative action. While you cannot advertise for these factors, you have a right to a "wish list." Also, knowing whom you most want to attract will aid in selecting where you will look for candidates.

Be sure your preferences are based on benefits derived from having certain types of volunteers (such as: involving ex-clients will bring us a new perspective), and not on preconceptions that may be based on prejudice (such as: older people have nothing better to do and so wouldn't mind this job). We will return to this important topic when we discuss diversity in Chapter 11.

Two Special Cases

This chapter has outlined how to approach the most common form of volunteer job design: creating specific roles for volunteers to meet pre-identified needs. However, there will be times when someone offers a skill you had not expected. How to react to such opportunities is discussed in Chapter 9 when we examine the things that happen when you are face-to-face with a prospect.

Finally, not every organization will want to be as formal as we have been assuming here (though I sincerely hope that you do not confuse structure and clarity with bureaucracy!). I will present a section called "Throwing Out the Rules" in Chapter 11, as a technique to be more welcoming to a wider range of prospective volunteers. The reason it's not in this chapter is that you're not ready for it yet! The *decision* to throw out the rules can only be made if you have rules from which to deviate. Start with the approach in this chapter and then be as flexible as you need to be.

Why People Volunteer ...and Don't

People volunteer for a wide variety of reasons. Some motives are altruistic in that they involve a desire to help others, or philanthropic, in that they are for the public good. There are even indications that involving oneself in the greater community is a natural human need, and that those who volunteer are actually healthier than those who do not.

It has been popular for some time to refer to the psychologist Abraham Maslow's "Hierarchy of Needs" to explain volunteer motivation. I have been itching for just as long to debunk that reference! Maslow theorized a pyramid of five human needs, in which the base is "physiological" (food, shelter, etc.), moving up to "safety" (secure from harm), then to "social" (the need to be liked), on to "esteem" (need to be valued), and finally "self-actualization" (being freed from all other needs to pursue personal happiness). Using Maslow, we conclude that people only volunteer when they reach the "top" of the chart—as an indicator of self-actualization. The theory goes that, at the bottom of the chart, people who are concerned with basic survival needs such as food and shelter are not able to volunteer. Poppycock!

An enormous amount of volunteering is directly concerned with *finding* food and shelter. Poor people do help one another; the first colonists did build their homes cooperatively; food co-ops and tenant unions involve members in self-help efforts. Being concerned for *oneself* does not have to mean *selfishness*. As we'll discuss later, a good number of social service organizations make a point of involving clients as "participant-volunteers." Such volunteers are best able to understand the problems being addressed and—relevant to the Maslow theory—it *builds* self-esteem to be a partner in, rather than a recipient of, services.

Some interpret Maslow to mean that people who are concerned with personal survival needs are unlikely to be motivated to volunteer for a cause unrelated to the basics. So trying to recruit a homeless person to be active with an environmental group or a museum might be wasted effort. But even this seemingly self-evident logic has been challenged by such programs as those that recruit low-income neighbors to paint murals or plant trees. Giving of oneself is a human need and being seen by others as a "resource" instead of as a charity case can be very important. Use your judgement, of course, but do not make unwarranted assumptions about people's abilities, interests, or dreams.

For those who want to read what scholars and researchers have been studying about volunteer motivations, the literature is growing. Unfortunately, much of the work starts with the puzzling approach of "what could possibly make these people do volunteer work anyway?" So, after painstaking statistical analysis, the researchers end up proving what we in the field knew anecdotally all along: there are *many* motivators for volunteering.

While most of the researchers are sociologists or psychologists, the subject of philanthropic motivation is also being examined by academics in fields such as religion and philosophy. In *Virtuous Giving* (Indiana University Press, 1994), applied ethicist Mike W. Martin urges volunteerism practitioners to see voluntary service in the broader context of human virtues and community ideals. All of this may seem intellectual or arcane, but it is helpful to develop a philosophic—even a moral—basis for why you expect people to give of themselves.

For you as a recruiter, the fact that volunteers have multiple motivations means that you will not be able to rely on one or two standard "grabbers" to turn prospects into recruits. Because different people will be enticed by different things, you will have to vary your approach all the time. Even the same assignment will not necessarily be attractive to each volunteer for the same reasons.

But the good news is that everybody has a "button" that can be pushed! The challenge is to spark the flame in each prospective volunteer so that she or he can become enthusiastic in a unique way.

On the following page are just a *few* of the reasons real-life volunteers give for doing actual volunteer work. See how many of these are applicable to you personally or to the volunteers already in your organization. I have been building this list through responses of participants in my recruitment workshops for many years, even outside North America. These reasons seem universal; volunteerism colleagues in South America and Europe identify the same motivators.

You will quickly note that some of the motivations shown could be considered "selfish" because they give something back to the volunteer. It is just fine to benefit from volunteering. In fact, the most successful form of volunteering is an *exchange* —when the giver and the recipient both come away with something positive. This makes voluntary service less an act of "charity" (based on the paternalistic attitude "we who have so much must give to those who have so little"), and more of a positive experience for everyone concerned.

In some situations, the lines between volunteer and recipient blur so that it is hard to tell who is who. If a group of seven-year-olds visits a senior center after school, bringing a welcome diversion but also getting help with homework, does it matter whether the youngsters or the elders are the "volunteers"? This concept might be very helpful

to you as a recruiter. After all, your job is to *meet needs*. Perhaps the best possible scenario is one in which all parties involved contribute resources and everyone benefits in some way.

Diagnosing the List

Examine the list further and you will see that some of the reasons indicate why someone is ready for volunteer work *in general* (free time on their hands, new to the neighborhood), while others point to why a *specific* opportunity might appeal. In the latter case, people are drawn either to the client group you serve (children, seniors, the deaf) or to the cause itself (fighting illiteracy, crime prevention). These volunteers might be open to doing a wide variety of tasks, so long as they have the chance to work with children or on behalf of cancer research.

On the other hand, some of the motivations are not connected to who is being served but to what the job itself is asking of the volunteer. Thus a calligrapher might happily make certificates for ten different agencies, all serving different groups, so long as the volunteer work involves pen and ink. Students who want to test their classroom learning may also be attracted to any agency that gives them that chance—and something on their résumé.

Note that this is an important point about *assumptions*. Someone does *not* have to "burn" to support your cause before joining you to be of help. He or she does *not* have to be a subscriber or audience member to be of help with your newsletter.

Another conclusion from the list of reasons why people volunteer is that few people are motivated by only one thing. More often it is a cluster of motivations that eventually make them select your opportunity over others. For example, I may want to help mentally retarded teenagers, but am also delighted at the chance to use my creative skills by accepting the volunteer job of crafts instructor with this client group.

You may find some of the motivators to be negative (feeling pressured or doing it for the benefits provided). Some reasons people volunteer are indeed problematic. But if we agree that most people act on a cluster of motives, we have to hope

Why People Volunteer

(just a few possible motivations)

- To feel needed
- To share skills
- For a change of pace
- To get to know a new community or neighborhood
- To help someone
- Because a family member or friend pressured them
- To gain leadership skills
- To get a change from being a leader
- To act out a fantasy
- To do their civic duty
- To earn academic credit
- To be with people who are different than themselves
- To keep busy
- The agency is geographically accessible
- To do something with a friend or family member
- To learn the truth
- To do one's share
- To see that resources are well allocated
- For recognition
- To make new friends
- To explore a career
- Parenthood
- To demonstrate commitment to a cause or belief
- To help a family member
- As therapy
- To do something different than their daily job
- For fun!!!
- For religious reasons
- To keep skills alive
- To repay a debt
- As an excuse to do something they love

- To donate their professional skills
- As a family tradition
- To be able to criticize without personal jeopardy
- Because there is no one else to do it
- To get the meals, transportation, or other benefits
- To assure progress
- To protect clients from an institution
- To feel good
- To have an impact
- Because their boss expects it
- To be part of a team
- To learn something new
- To be an advocate
- To gain status
- To get out of the house
- For freedom of schedule
- Because they were asked
- Because of who did the asking
- To test themselves
- For escape
- To become an "insider"
- To be an agent of change
- Because of their personal experience with a cause or problem
- Guilt
- Because of interest in or concern for the particular client group
- To gain access to services for themselves
- To be challenged
- To experiment with new ways of doing something
- As an alternative to giving money
- To be a watchdog
- To feel proud
- To stand up and be counted

some of their other reasons are more positive—or that we can help these volunteers to find satisfaction in the work despite themselves! On the other hand, after an interview, we may need to screen out those people whose initial reasons for wanting to join have potential for interfering with their ability to do the work well.

Note, too, that motivations change as people move into different stages of life, though it is hard to generalize about when someone may feel lonely or be eager to learn something new.

Finally, the reasons why people *remain* on the job are often quite different from what grabbed them in the first place. Your job as a volunteer recruiter is to capture their enthusiasm initially.

Fun

When you examine the list of reasons why people volunteer, you will see that "fun" is on the list. Sometimes we in the volunteer world get so caught up in following the model of the world of paid work that we forget that volunteering is essentially a *recreational* activity! People can only volunteer in their discretionary time, when they are not committed to their livelihood, family or other obligations. So when you recruit, you are not competing with a paying job. Rather, you are asking people to give up time with their own family or friends, time they have to do what they find relaxing. Your real competition is golf, going to the movies, driving the kids to and from the soccer game, and taking a nap!

So volunteering at your organization better have some social, enjoyable aspect to it. This does not mean you can't ask people to work hard as volunteers or to do projects independently. But there should be some pleasure in the task itself, in meeting the others who will be participating, or in the sense of accomplishment at the end. For some of you, the word "fun" can actually be used openly. If you are recruiting for a cultural arts group, outdoor facility, or any type of organization that people might think of as a free time activity, why not play it up? For example, the National Ski Patrol knows full well that its members gladly patrol the slopes in exchange for the pleasure of skiing more often with less guilt.

Even the most mundane of tasks can be made

appealing if the "recreational model" is applied. So instead of begging people to grit their teeth and clean up a vacant lot, add a "song fest" and make it an event. The same holds true for that much-maligned yet vital task of envelope stuffing. I maintain there's real potential for an "Executive Envelope Stuffing Circle," open by invitation only to the top CEOs in town, with the promise of giving participants three hours in a room with their peers—without telephones or other interruptions. Add some croissants and—voila!—a new recruitment pitch!

The recreational model also leads to creative approaches to recruitment. Why not tap into the desire of working women to spend more time with their friends by recruiting friends *together* to volunteer as a team—or families who want to find ways to develop their relationships? Ivan Scheier notes that we might occasionally recruit by pointing out that "we give you all these chances to have fun and we don't even charge admission!"

In all-volunteer associations, the social element is vital. People join groups if they think they will make friends with other members and will enjoy the various activities—including service projects.

What Do You Offer?

As you look over the list of motivators, think about which ones might be most applicable to those who might volunteer with your organization. (You might even interview some current volunteers to ask them directly.) More importantly, consider the job descriptions you have developed for volunteers and identify what might turn someone on about them. What are the "perks"?

If you can't answer this question, go back and redesign the job descriptions!

Why People Don't Volunteer

Recognize that not everyone is a prospect for you. No matter how perfect your recruitment campaign, your cause or the things you need volunteers to do, you will simply not appeal to everyone. And that is fine. After all, there are hundreds of worthwhile agencies in every community and there should be enough volunteers to go around.

Some people will never want to volunteer in a prison, while the folks who gravitate to helping offenders might well abhor the thought of building a bird blind in the forest. That's why there's chocolate and vanilla, and it's why you won't win 'em all.

Second, some people are not likely candidates because they do not qualify for your program or because the logistics are all wrong. If you need a driver on Tuesdays and a prospective volunteer is busy every Tuesday, you just don't have a match.

Finally, there are some people who simply won't volunteer. They may have preconceived notions about volunteering itself. They may consider it demeaning or not politically correct. They may hold to the belief that "if it's important to do, it should be paid for." They may be turned off by the image of volunteers as do-gooders, or women, or whatever. You cannot convert everyone to embrace volunteering. The best you can do is consistently present a positive image of being a volunteer with *your* organization.

The best thing you can do for yourself in recruitment is to enable people to *screen themselves out* before they even take your time. You do this by being as clear as possible in what you tell them while you recruit. More on this in Chapter 9. But after you have ruled out the foregoing three categories of refusals, the question still remains: why do some possibly qualified candidates turn you down?

First, be sure that you have, in fact, *been* turned down. The number one reason why people do not volunteer is:

They do not feel they were asked!

Publicity is *not* recruitment. Putting up a poster or using your newsletter may inform people of your volunteer needs, but folks may not realize that they themselves are candidates. Strange but true. And here is another truth:

Most people do not say "no"; they simply never knew you wanted them to say "yes."

This should be reassuring as you step out to recruit! In Section II, we will examine the best ways to extend the invitation to volunteer.

Real Turn-downs

We have already discussed why it is important for you as a recruiter to understand why people volunteer. But it is equally vital to consider what might stop someone from accepting your invitation to join in. By identifying the obstacles to volunteer recruitment, you can either change the negative factors into positive ones or you can acknowledge concerns before a prospective volunteer raises them.

Distinguish valid concerns from myths and stereotypes. Be willing to consider that there could be some genuine obstacles for a prospective volunteer. For example:

* There is no public transportation close to your facility or the parking situation is bad or costly. In rural communities, the distances between people and between your site and other destinations may be great—or insurmountable—for someone without a car.

* The work itself is repetitive, physically difficult, or taken for granted.

* Your schedules do not match. Not only might the prospective volunteer be unable to serve during your office hours, but other timing might also be a problem. You allow the volunteer to work evenings or weekends, but the initial screening interview may be offered only from nine to five on weekdays. Or new volunteer orientations may be scheduled only in the mornings—or only in the evenings. Ditto for training sessions, especially if they are offered only once or twice a year at set intervals. So the volunteer has the burden of juggling his or her available time before having any satisfaction from the work itself.

* There are actual and hidden financial costs. Are there out-of-pocket expenses expected of every volunteer such as transportation, uniforms, meals, or child care? Comparatively small costs such as parking meters or vending machine snacks can add up over time for volunteers on fixed income or youthful allowances. Not so obvious may be the need for a volunteer to purchase work-

appropriate clothing, subtle pressure to contribute to holiday funds, or feeling obligated to buy something for a client (which may actually not be something you encourage at all). Examine the annual amount of money volunteers spend on your behalf. Can any of this be reimbursed or covered in some other way? If not, you may be inadvertently sending the message that only well-to-do volunteers need apply.

Other concerns may be less tangible:

- The problems you are addressing seem overwhelming.
- There was a negative situation involving your agency in the past. (See Chapter 4 on image.)
- Long-time volunteers already on board have strong personalities and may be incompatible with the new people you are trying to recruit.
- In the past, most of your volunteers have been different from the prospective candidate in sex, race, or background.
- Fear of seeing something distasteful or frightening.
- Fear that the work will be too difficult (fear of failure).

Risk and Liability

A lot of attention has been paid recently to fears about volunteer risk and liability. As with anything else, the risks of volunteering are both real and imagined. Whether or not a volunteer assignment is risky depends on the specific tasks to be done and the ability or skill of the volunteer doing them. Obviously the odds of an injury are greater if a volunteer is clearing out a forest nature trail than if that same person is entering data on an office computer. Similarly, the chance a volunteer might be sued by a client varies with the type of service being provided.

As a volunteer program manager, you should be informed about risk and liability and you should make sure your organization carries whatever insurance coverage may be necessary. And you should practice all the techniques of good risk management. There are some excellent resources to help you with this.[1] As a recruiter, your job is to explain the most likely causes of accidents or liability, neither downplaying nor over-emphasizing this issue. You should also explain how the organization supports volunteers to minimize the chances of something going wrong.

Keep in mind that everything we do in life—and in our lawsuit-happy culture—carries risk. We all make choices every day as to the liability to which we will expose ourselves. Almost by definition, many of the causes that volunteers support require working in less-than-ideal settings, in situations that may compromise personal security. The volunteer candidate who is overly concerned about insurance questions may ultimately be the wrong prospect for your organization. (Just be sure that the volunteer is really "overly concerned" and not that your risk management is not properly developed.)

The Implications of Gravy

A number of years ago I conducted a workshop in a rural area on the subject of volunteer recruitment. As I led the group in examining why some people are reluctant to volunteer, one participant observed: "People don't like to volunteer for us because they don't like to get the back seats of their cars dirty." She went on to explain that she ran a homebound meal delivery program that was required to use a certain type of food container with a lid that did not fit properly. Therefore, gravy splattered out from the container and onto the back seats of the volunteer drivers' cars.

The rest of the group and I questioned why these containers could not be replaced or fixed, but the woman repeated that she had no options to make such changes. Then another participant raised her hand. "We had the same problem," she shared, "and now what we do is send the gravy out in thermos bottles. Not only does this keep the volunteers' cars clean, but our clients receive gravy that is still hot."

I was delighted. We had networked people from the same state and found an easy and inexpensive solution to the first woman's problem. She, however, reacted without enthusiasm: "Oh, we could never afford thermos bottles."

It was then that I shocked everyone by saying: "Then I suppose you don't deserve to recruit any volunteers."

In effect, my trainee was saying that she would rather continue her search to find volunteers willing to have the backs of their cars slopped up with gravy than fix the real problem of the food container. After all, this was a rural area with no more than ten to fifteen delivery routes per day. What could the cost have been to budget for the purchase of sufficient thermos bottles? Was there really no merchant or civic-minded person who might donate fifteen thermos bottles to this worthwhile cause—if asked? Could not volunteers themselves provide one thermos bottle for their own route?

By the end of the day, all was well. The group had recovered from the blow of my honesty and the woman had acknowledged that what she had expressed as a volunteer recruitment problem was, in fact, an *institutional obstacle* that prospective volunteers recognized as too high a price to pay for the privilege of volunteering.

Does your organization have a "gravy problem"? We have already discussed some of the reasons why people may be reluctant to volunteer in your setting. The gravy story is an example of a situation in which it was unrealistic to expect volunteers to accept the assignment as offered. There are other ways we place unreasonable demands on volunteers. We may want the recording secretary to take minutes, type them personally, and mail them out—all from home. This implies that the volunteer not only knows how to take minutes, but has the clerical skills and the necessary equipment available to do the entire job. Another volunteer may be expected to handle all the financial and administrative recordkeeping for a special event, and also to recruit other volunteers to help on the day of the program. This requires "left side/ right side of the brain" talents which may be contradictory. Some volunteers are turned off because they continuously feel inadequate to do the whole job and unrecognized for the sub-tasks they can do well.

In some settings, it is not enough that volunteers give their time in direct service. In addition, all volunteers are expected to "join" the organization or some special group such as an auxiliary.

This may entail yet another cash expense, and also carries the burden of additional obligations, mailings, and still more meeting invitations. Evaluate what the purpose of such memberships really is. Is there a clear benefit to the volunteer? Or is the real motive to add to the membership rolls of a group that is struggling to keep current? As more and more volunteers seek short-term, product-oriented assignments, the concept of membership (which almost always operates on an annual basis) may have little relevance.

"Diversity" in your volunteer corps is an ambitious, yet important, goal. While most organizations are genuine in their desire to attract volunteers of multi-racial and multicultural backgrounds, they do not expect to change the way they do business. In other words, organizations want volunteers (and employees, too) to look diverse, but to do the same work in the same ways as in the past. Volunteers who are different in background, income, or education may also bring new approaches to their assignments. For example, working "by committee" is a very traditional, Anglo-Saxon way to organize people. A Latino neighborhood group or African-American church guild might operate with a different structure and be equally productive. How open is your organization to alternative methods of getting work done? Do you adapt to the needs of volunteers or expect volunteers to adapt to you? Is there room for compromise?

There are other diversity issues as well. For example, there may be tension between new volunteers and veteran volunteers if the newcomers are much younger or come from the corporate world. The members of an "advisory council" recruited for their expertise may soon find that no one actually wants any "advice." See Chapter 11 for much more on the subject of diversity.

So the next time you have difficulty recruiting volunteers (in general or for a particular assignment), analyze the situation carefully. It may be your recruiting materials or "pitch" that can be improved. Perhaps you can be better at targeting your audience. But also check for gravy stains! When people do not want to join your effort, they may be telling you something about your organization. Fix the real problem and recruitment may take care of itself.

"I Don't Have the Time"

The most common reason given when a prospective volunteer says no is lack of time. Adults certainly are busy, but we often suspect that this is an excuse. Before you conclude that such people are uncaring or apathetic, consider that they may already be committed to the maximum level with other community or family responsibilities. Or, the timing of your request may be awful: a child or parent may be sick, their legal bar exam may be looming in a month, they may have just accepted a new job with much responsibility.

On the other hand, the phrase, "sorry, I'm too busy," may be code for: "what you just asked me to do has too little interest for me to make time in my life for it." As a recruiter, you need to be sure which factor is at work. We'll come back to this in Chapter 9 when we look at how to approach people one-to-one.

Address the Concerns

Just as you need to diagnose why people might be attracted to become a volunteer with your organization, you should carefully identify the obstacles. Which can you address? For example, is there flexibility in the assignment schedule so that you can accommodate a greater diversity of time availability? Can you assign volunteers in teams so as to minimize fears about personal safety? Can you reimburse out-of-pocket costs? Will you provide training? Is there insurance to cover accidents?

Some of these strategies for minimizing the possible concerns of prospective volunteers involve money. An organization's commitment to the value of volunteer efforts is demonstrated by the readiness to budget appropriately for such participation. The question is not necessarily whether there are funds available *today* for insurance, volunteer out-of-pocket expenses, or other items. The real litmus test of commitment is whether or not an organization is willing to plan ahead for such expenses and to *fundraise* when necessary to find the money in the future. Without some access to "enabling funds," you may not be able to recruit all the people you feel would make the best volunteers.

Be open to the wide diversity of prospective volunteers who may well be attracted to you. On the other hand, don't spend too much time trying to recruit the wrong people.

One last caution: avoid speaking with "forked tongue." If you tell people that volunteers in your organization meet real needs, give important input, or have fun—be sure you are telling the truth! If your recruitment message is enthusiastic and motivating but the things volunteers do are dull and limited, the shock of reality will make volunteers leave. And then you'll be out recruiting again and again in an endless cycle.

---

[1]See Charles Tremper and Gwynne Kostin, *No Surprises: Controlling Risks in Volunteer Programs* (Washington, DC: Nonprofit Risk Management Center, 1993).

The Power of Image

It often surprises me that volunteer recruiters expect people to sign up with organizations about which they know nothing. How can someone be eager to serve an organization that is a mystery? For this reason we need to spend some time on the subject of image.

The preceding chapters have dealt with volunteer recruitment in something of a vacuum—we have considered all of the in-house tasks within the domain of the volunteer program leader. But volunteers are a part of the whole organization and the organization exists in the community. Public perception about the organization therefore affects volunteer recruitment. In this chapter we will explore some important questions that may require the involvement of the agency's executive director, board, or other staff members if change is necessary. For our focus on volunteer recruitment, the challenge is to understand the public context within which recruiting takes place and to adapt our presentations accordingly.

In all honesty it should also be noted that there are times in which an organization's inability to recruit volunteers is a reflection of major problems with the acceptance of the value of the organization. People may be telling you that they don't believe in what you are doing, or in how you are doing it. Or times may have changed and the public perceives you as producing buggy whips—other causes are now more important. This is why it is vital to consider the questions in this chapter. Is your recruiting problem a symptom of something more serious? Or can you conclude that people support your work and would volunteer if your outreach efforts improve?

The Connection to Public Relations

Volunteer recruitment is inseparable from agency public relations. The better known an organization, the easier it is for the recruiter to begin. Unless, of course, what is known about the organization is *negative*. More on that in a moment.

Unless you are on the staff of one of the groups we call "household names" (such as Girl Scouts, the YMCA, or the Red Cross), never assume that the public is aware of your existence. Even if you are with one of the "household name" groups, do not assume the public is correctly informed or updated about your work. Many women know the Girl Scouts from twenty-five years ago when they themselves were Scouts —how relevant are such memories to today's volunteer activities?

So the first challenge you have is to introduce your organization—briefly but captivatingly—to the listener, reader, or target of your recruitment campaign. You will be helped immeasurably if your organization has a public relations effort underway at all times. Before you design your volunteer recruitment effort, study:

- What publicity has the agency received lately? If none, recognize the absence.

- If there has been publicity, was it good or bad? Did it relate directly to the effort for which you need volunteers?

- What do the organization's printed materials say? Are they welcoming?

- Do the organization's materials mention that volunteers are part of the service delivery team? Or are volunteers an "invisible" resource? If the latter, don't assume the public even knows you have volunteers.

- What kinds of fundraising does your organization do? Are there many mailings that go out all year? To whom? Might this help or hurt your recruitment for donated *time*? Might there be a way to mesh (or at least coordinate) such public outreach efforts?

- Is the only time people hear from your organization when you want something?

- If you sponsor special events, how are these publicized and what types of volunteers are involved with them?

- How welcoming is your building and its entrance? Do visitors pass through brightly decorated halls? Are they confronted by grumpy security guards?

- What happens when people telephone your agency? Does your voice mail system work? Is there a live, friendly voice at all times, occasionally, or never?

It is fascinating to examine how the public forms an opinion about you. The little things count!

Much of the time you may not be in control of your organization's public relations efforts. There may be other agency staff whose main job is public relations, or fundraising, or customer relations. You probably do not supervise the telephone receptionist or other employees who set the tone for your organization on a daily basis. But you still have to recognize and deal with the image that is projected because it has a direct effect on volunteer recruitment and retention.

Work at making volunteers visible throughout your organization. Request the use of a public bulletin board and keep it decorated with news and photographs about the accomplishments of volunteers. Not just birthdays! Focus on achievements in meeting goals or doing something innovative. Be sure to put up a pocket clearly marked, "Interested in Joining Us?," that contains flyers a prospect can take for more details about becoming a volunteer.

Similarly, talk with the editor of your organization's newsletter and see if you can develop a regular column about volunteers or if a feature story might be planned. You may find that the reason volunteers have been ignored so far is that the editor has no idea what to say! It is up to you to make coverage "newsworthy" to your in-house editor, just as when approaching the mass media.

If your walk-through of your setting leads to the conclusion that it feels unwelcoming, there may be little you can do to renovate the physical look. But turn the negative into a tool. Prepare people coming to interview that the building does not reflect on the warmth of the people. Use humor. During the 1970's, I was the director of volunteers for the Family Court of Philadelphia. My office was located in what had once been a detention area—and still had bars on the windows. First, an enterprising volunteer decorated a few of them with paint and vines. Then, during my interview if I saw a candidate eyeing the bars, I'd say: "So, you thought volunteering here was voluntary, huh?"

The truth was that some people were probably scared off by the setting. That was O.K. They were likely to be unrealistic about the justice field anyway. But others could be made to feel comfortable despite the grim room.

Diagnosing Your Image

When you ask someone to volunteer, you are asking him or her to affiliate with you. This means that people, whether consciously or not, will assess whether your organization has an image that matches their self-image. Put another way, prospective volunteers must be able to *picture themselves* working with you.

There are several mental pictures at work. First, there is the image of the overall organization. Consider these questions:

- How long have you been in existence?
- Has this history been one of continuous success and growth or have there been public setbacks, funding problems, changes in administration?
- What is your general reputation in the community?

- What are your major sources of funding? (And what, in turn, is the image of those funders?)
- Have you been involved in any controversy in the past few years? In your distant past? (People's memories are amazingly long.)
- Why *haven't* you been involved in controversy? (Might your image be one of playing it safe and traditional?)
- Are you perceived as rich? As struggling?
- Do you own or occupy nice quarters?
- Is your neighborhood perceived as safe or not?
- What is the age of your staff?
- What is the sex of your staff?
- What is the racial and ethnic makeup of your staff?
- What professions are represented on the staff?
- How long a waiting period is there for service?
- How friendly are your reception desk staff and your telephone operators?
- How visible are volunteers currently to the public?
- What is the demographic make-up of the volunteer corps? (For example, if you are now actively seeking male volunteers, is the image of your organization one of women and is this correct or a stereotype?)
- How often do you change anything? Are you perceived as open to suggestions? Flexible?
- Whom do you serve? (This may be a trick question!)

There are no right or wrong answers to the above questions, but before you can design any volunteer recruitment campaign, you must have an accurate assessment of how the public perceives your organization. Is this perception accurate or not? Is this perception positive or negative?

The clearer you become about the image of your organization, the better you will be at targeting the types of people who would feel comfortable in affiliating with you. Build on any positive public perceptions—show people how volunteer-

ing continues a tradition of respected service. Make a great reputation work for you! Conversely, by understanding that some elements of your image may be potentially negative, you can address the possible concerns of prospective volunteers from the beginning.

A negative image is not insurmountable. In fact, some volunteers are attracted by the idea that they can problem-solve or counteract a prejudicial situation. During my years with the Philadelphia Family Court, half the crime in Pennsylvania occurred in Philadelphia and half the crime in Philadelphia was perpetrated by juveniles. *No one* in Philadelphia thought the Court was doing a good job of dealing with delinquents or with families in domestic crisis. When I went out to recruit volunteers, I had to understand that my audiences were, at best, skeptical and, at worst, hostile. Could I act as though I already had support? Of course not. But I could begin my presentations with thoughts like: "I'll bet you never expected to hear someone from the Court asking for help," or "Even if you want the system to change, we still have 17,000 teenagers going through it right now and you can make a difference for a few of them." You get the point.

What If You Are a Government Agency?

One of the stereotypes about volunteering is that it takes place only in nonprofit agencies. Not true. Volunteers are involved in literally thousands of government agencies at the municipal, county, state, and national levels. Just consider such settings as public schools, parks and forests, courts and prisons, Veterans Hospitals, etc. Yet some people may believe that *taxes* are their way of supporting government services. Their image of government might see recruiting volunteers as a form of "double dipping" into the pockets/time of citizens.

On the other hand, others are genuinely attracted to the concept of volunteering as a way to keep taxes under control. They may perceive the opportunity to volunteer within government as an expression of participatory democracy. In fact, some might argue that it is the right of citizens to become involved in the monitoring and delivering of community services by public agencies.

Much of the time, people do not distinguish volunteering for a nonprofit agency from volunteering for a government agency. If someone is interested in helping in a hospital, whether the funding source is the county or private donors is usually irrelevant. Today the funding streams are so blurred that it is sometimes hard to draw the lines between public and private institutions anyway. Just be aware that some prospective volunteers may have feelings about the government issue and be prepared to discuss the question honestly.

What If You Are a For-Profit or Proprietary Business?

A growing number of for-profit businesses are entering the service field. Hospitals and nursing homes are increasingly profit-making, as are some prisons, counseling services, and recreation providers. Government is subcontracting for services from businesses in an attempt to be cost-effective. Further muddying the water is the emergence of "holding companies" formed from agency or institutional mergers and resulting in both nonprofit and for-profit ventures under the same governing body. It is getting harder and harder to distinguish charities from businesses.

Is it wrong to expect volunteers to help a for-profit venture? Some say yes. They take the position that volunteers should be asked to donate their time to organizations benefitting the public good, not to add to the profit of individuals (even though these goals are not mutually exclusive). Often this opinion is based on a superficial understanding of the role of volunteers and, if you are the director of volunteers in a for-profit setting, you will need to be able to articulate the reasons why it is quite valid and valuable for volunteers to be involved.

First, you can note that businesses of all types routinely provide placements for student interns. The "exchange" of experience for the student's work is considered legitimate compensation. But this is still a form of volunteering. Second, there are a number of programs designed expressly to recruit volunteers to help businesses succeed. The most well known is the Small Business Administration's SCORE (Senior Corps of Retired Executives), which provides volunteers with business expertise to work with new and minority business owners. If volunteers can be asked to increase the profit-making potential of manufacturing, sales, and service companies, why is it farfetched to recruit volunteers to participate in businesses providing the same client services as some not-for-profits?

The key is to distinguish between volunteer assignments that assist "the company" from those that assist the *recipients of service*. No business (or nonprofit, for that matter) is ever going to provide the personal touch that volunteers offer to individual patients or clients. If you are in a proprietary setting, you are well-advised to develop a written statement of philosophy about the role of volunteers, explaining that they do not help the business to spend less (or hire fewer employees), but rather volunteers strengthen services to the agency's consumers. Your list of available volunteer job descriptions should reflect this.

The point, as always, is to be honest with prospective volunteers about your source of funding and to recognize that people will react to your sponsorship based on their image of business, government or nonprofits.

What If You Are Affiliated with a Sponsoring Organization?

Yet another possible type of sponsorship is being an affiliate or branch of a national organization or large local agency. Even if your particular affiliate is independently incorporated and has its own board, if you carry a name such as Big Brothers/Big Sisters, March of Dimes, or the YMCA, the public will link you with any other affiliate anywhere. This means that you carry both the halo and the burden of any reputation developed nationally. People will transfer to you all the feelings they may have from experiences with your counterparts in other cities. Again, this may work for or against your recruiting effort. Use any positive attitudes to your advantage and find ways to distinguish your local activities from those of your colleagues if you need to achieve some separate identity.

Similarly, if your sponsor is something like the Jewish Federation, the Hispanic League, or a large university, you will have to recognize and accommodate your sponsor's image along with your specific program. Do people know of the connection? Do they understand why this sponsor is funding your program? Does the affiliation mean that participation is exclusive? For example, can a non-Christian be a volunteer with Lutheran Family Services? Explain whatever is necessary to welcome people as volunteers.

Diagnosing Related Images

Connected to how your organization is perceived is the public's image of your *client group* (or your consumers or audience). You need to consider these types of questions:

- Do you serve the public at large? If so, does everyone make use of your services or just some segments of the community . . . and which ones?

- If you have a targeted client base, is it upper, middle or lower class?

- What stereotypes might the public have about the people you serve?

- Is this group generally accepted as needy (example: abandoned babies) or are there controversies about the target group (example: homeless drug addicts)?

Do not assume that volunteers will not want to work with a "difficult" client base! "Difficult" is in the eye of the beholder. As we covered in Chapter 3, some people love children, others prefer seniors, or vice versa. Some people would hate working with delinquents but feel drawn to work with the mentally retarded, and vice versa. Some people want to enjoy "clean" community service, such as in support of the arts, but others feel that genuine service means being in the trenches with the most needy people.

The key is to describe your clients/consumers so that prospective volunteers can decide if they will feel comfortable in working with them. For example, you can address possible stereotypes by showing slides or photographs (you'll need to get clients to sign consent forms to be pictured). Many nursing homes find that people incorrectly assume all residents are bedridden or in wheelchairs all day. A set of slides showing the dining room at lunchtime effectively counters that assumption and shows that volunteers will be interacting with many different types of residents.

Recognize, too, that people infer things from whom you serve. If you are a Women's Center, do you want any men as volunteers? Is it necessary to be bilingual to volunteer with the Cuban Concilio? Without clarification, prospective volunteers may wrongly assume they are not welcome or qualified.

Another image issue is the *service you provide* or the *cause you support*:

- Is it controversial?

- Is it understandable?

- Can it be described easily?

- Have you had any visible successes?

- Is your mission perceived as achievable at all (world peace) or far in the future (ending hunger)?

- How many other organizations are doing the same or similar things? What makes you different? Why are you different?

- Who are your allies?

From a recruitment point of view, it is helpful to identify your "competition." If you help recovering drug addicts, what other organizations in town work with this client base and what do they offer for volunteers to do?

Once again, the point of all this diagnosis is to strengthen your recruitment presentation. Without introducing negative thoughts to your audience, you want to anticipate possible negative responses and counteract them—or to build on positive feelings already at work. There are three ways you can approach possible hostility or misinformation, depending of course on the nature of the problem:

— *Acceptance:* acknowledge that there has been some controversy and note that it is the price your organization has paid for being true to its beliefs, or explain how things have changed since the original situation occurred in the past.

— *Challenge assumptions:* be willing to engage in some nonaggressive confrontation, "setting the record straight" and noting that people have heard rumors rather than truth.

— *Humor:* demonstrate that your organization has moved past the negative situation by making light of it (but never mocking the person who raises the question) or telling an anecdote that shows its lighter side.

You won't win 'em all. But then again, not everyone is the right volunteer for you.

Ultimately, each person will make a personal assessment of whether or not your organization is worth his or her volunteer effort. There will be many variables as to why someone selects your organization with which to volunteer, but the initial attraction comes from each candidate's perception of your image.

The Image of Volunteering

There is one more image question that definitely has an impact on a volunteer recruiter: the public's perception of "volunteering." And this is being affected by various trends in the volunteerism field that are producing new (and sometimes conflicting) vocabulary.

As a culture, we have contradictory views of the value of volunteering. On the one hand, we esteem the heroes and heroines who take risks to fight for what is right. We also honor those who come forward in times of crisis to fill sandbags against a flood or clean up after an earthquake. These Good Samaritan efforts are universally praised and accepted as representing the best of "community participation."

But we also denigrate the person who "works for nothing" as a "sucker." Our folklore ridicules "do-gooders" who can be exploited and who ultimately do little good. Because we measure personal worth by such external criteria as earning power, volunteer activities are seen as nice but really a diversion from the road to success.

How are volunteers viewed within your organization? One clue is the degree of responsibility given to volunteers. If all the assignments are low-risk, window-dressing sorts of tasks, then the organization perpetuates the image of volunteers as amateurs who are essentially helpers. Or, by in-

volving volunteers in roles at every level, you can demonstrate that volunteers are vital contributors to the basic services of the organization.

Stereotypes about who volunteers abound. One image held by many is that a "volunteer" is a little old lady in a flowered hat and tennis shoes. Many believe that most volunteers are female, white, and wealthy. While the data contradict such preconceptions, you may be fighting a tradition in your field or setting that fits the stereotype. So if for the past twenty years your auxiliary has been 98% female, do not be surprised that the public thinks your recruitment campaign is not aimed at men (the reverse may be true for a volunteer fire-fighting company).

There are lots of other misconceptions about volunteering. Because early feminist doctrine condemned direct-service volunteering as keeping women in "second-class citizen" roles, some women resist what they perceive as "traditional" volunteering. Recognize that the feminist debate served to make everyone much more thoughtful about how we used—and abused—volunteer time, as well as to open the board room to both genders. And political or change-oriented volunteer service was always acknowledged as a positive activity for women.

Another misconception is that "volunteering takes paid jobs" or permits inadequate budgeting. This is the root of labor union resistance to volunteers and many people are justifiably concerned that employees be treated fairly. When the economy is bad or funding is scarce, some organizations do indeed begin to speak about volunteers as a low-cost "solution" to the crisis. I've already cautioned about this approach in Chapter 1. In the short term, volunteers may be part of a strategy for tiding an organization through hard times. But in the long term, history shows that volunteers have *created* more jobs than taken them. Volunteers are generally the very people who understand why full-time trained attention to a problem is needed. Learn about this ongoing process of paid job creation in *By the People: A History of Americans as Volunteers* (Ellis and Noyes, Jossey-Bass, 1990). Be aware, however, that people who strongly support labor unions can have prejudices against volunteers.

As a recruiter, you will be affected both by the

internal image of volunteers in your agency and by the mental image that prospective candidates have in their own minds about volunteers: do they picture themselves under this label?

Often, in fact, the problem is *language*. As we will discuss in the following chapter on trends and issues in volunteerism, what is "volunteering" and who is a "volunteer" are not universally-accepted truths. So if you are saying "join us as a volunteer" to someone who is looking for some "*pro bono work*" to do, you may never get your message across.

Consider the following words and phrases. What does each mean and how might it relate to the broader, umbrella concept of "volunteering"?

- —community service
- —*pro bono publico* work
- —activism
- —mutual aid
- —social concern
- —charity
- —barter
- —neighborliness
- —experiential learning
- —corporate social responsibility
- —unpaid staff
- —community resources
- —auxiliaries/friends groups
- —citizen participation
- —lay ministry
- —self-help
- —citizenship
- —public service
- —service-learning
- —internship
- —community involvement
- —any social "movement"
- —philanthropy
- —trustee
- —donor
- —member

As a recruiter, you may need to adapt your language to the ears of your listening audience. Whether or not a person responds to the label "volunteer" is hardly an indicator of whether or not s/he can be of help.

If you are with a Volunteer Center or other volunteer referral service, the issues of the image of volunteering and vocabulary choice are critical to any community-wide awareness effort you may undertake. See my book *Volunteer Centers: Gearing Up for the 1990s* (United Way of America, 1989) for suggestions on how to develop public visibility and advocacy for volunteerism.

Addressing All the Images

This chapter has raised some critical and complex issues, many beyond the purview of this book. But I hope you can see that, as a recruiter, you need to understand the context of your outreach efforts. Some organizations cannot be successful in volunteer recruitment until they deal with how they are perceived in the community. This may be the biggest gravy stain of all!

In no way am I implying that a negative image means you cannot find people to volunteer. But I do believe that your job is much harder if you are unaware of what people are thinking as you recruit. Sometimes it is actually easier to get volunteer cooperation when things are bad. The pitch of "we need you to help turn things around" can be very effective. What you want to avoid, however, is cheerily writing flyers and making speeches while your audience is muttering under its breath.

For most readers, however, your answers to the image questions in this chapter will reveal pluses as well as minuses. As with so many other things, it is probably helpful to convene a group of volunteers, a group of clients, and maybe a group of neighbors who have never volunteered with you and *ask them* how they would answer some of these questions. It might be a fascinating exercise. You may well discover that the public thinks highly of you even if they can't exactly tell you why. Use whatever good feelings are out there to build your recruitment efforts.

It may be a good idea to recruit some volunteers skilled in public relations to work with you as you develop new recruitment materials. Certainly you want to enlist the help of your organization's public relations director and development staff (if your agency is large enough to have these), since both have an equally vested interest in the messages that are sent to the community. At the very least, ask for some time with your adminis- trators to discuss how your volunteer recruiting efforts mesh with other agency outreach for clients and funding.

An aware recruiter is a successful recruiter!

Trends and Issues in Volunteerism

Volunteerism never occurs in a vacuum. If the economy or the population shifts, volunteering will reflect the changes just as does the job market, or the divorce rate, or any other aspect of society. So it is important for the volunteer recruiter to understand the trends and issues impacting on prospective volunteers at any given time. The trouble is that trends and issues change.

Almost everything in this book has stood the test of time and will probably hold true for quite a while to come. This chapter is a bit more risky. Some of the trends in 1994 may well continue for many years; others will be more transitory. Your crystal ball is as good as mine.

As with the preceding chapter on your image, the point here is to be as educated a recruiter as possible. Some of these trends suggest ways you might update or adapt volunteer job descriptions and therefore tap new talent pools. Other trends imply ways to tie recruiting to factors affecting your audience in other aspects of their lives—showing volunteering as a way to cope with changes happening anyway.

The following short descriptions are not meant to be complete or exhaustive, nor are they presented in order of importance. But these issues all have an impact on recruitment. We will refer to many of these trends again in later chapters. The best way to read this chapter is to see it as a model—a way to approach integrating your knowledge of current issues with what might affect your success in mobilizing people to volunteer.

Changing Vocabulary versus Real Change: "Community Service"

In the previous chapter we looked at the many different terms and phrases used to describe what we might generically label "volunteering." As already pointed out, in some cases the vocabulary issue is purely semantics. And as a recruiter, you must learn when to change your words in order to communicate effectively.

But some of the changing vocabulary reflects an evolution in categories of volunteering. Perhaps the most important new phrase is "community service" which, ironically, has two different applications. Since the 1970's, the courts have used "community service" to refer to the concept of requiring someone to give a certain number of hours of unpaid service to a community agency, either in lieu of a fine or incarceration, or in tandem with probation or parole. There was an understandable reluctance to use the word "volunteer" for a group of workers who were, in effect, being "punished" or providing restitution. There seemed to be little "voluntary" about it. Other terms for these programs include "court-ordered service" or "alternative sentencing."

If your community has a court-ordered community service program, consider whether or not your organization might make use of such workers. You can set guidelines as to the type of offense you are willing to accept and you can require a minimum number of hours or certain skills. For some types of volunteer assignments, court-ordered workers are ideal. And it is important to note that time has shown that in every community in which alternative sentencing has been tried, a percentage of the people forced to do community service has *continued* to do volunteer work after their required hours were completed.

In the 1980's the phrase "community service" was appropriated by the academic community to refer to school-based, usually curriculum-oriented, service projects by students. The term was consciously selected to differentiate the students' work from traditional "volunteering" for both valid and invalid reasons. The invalid reasons revolved around the continuing stereotype of volunteering as being "helper" work, amateur and nonessential. Faculty and students wanted to give quality service, based on expertise just learned in the classroom—hence the desire for a different name.

The other reason for rejecting the volunteer label was similar to the court-ordered problem. A growing number of colleges, high schools, and even lower grades have begun to *mandate* a certain number of hours of "community service" as a requirement for graduation. "Mandatory volunteering" is an oxymoron and so a new term was needed.

If you are unfamiliar with the developments in student community service, learn more. This is a growing arena and holds enormous potential for volunteer programs. The National and Community Service Act which I'll discuss in the next section provides a funding stream to support school-based service from Kindergarten through the twelfth grade. To tap the student audience, you will definitely need to speak their language. Some other terms you may hear are: experiential learning, service-learning, internship, and reflection opportunity. Faculty and students have come to recognize that their entry point into an agency is often going to be the volunteer program leader, even if they question the label "volunteer."

Keep in mind that different recruitment approaches are needed to tap formal academic internship programs versus campus student activity offices (we'll discuss this more in other chapters). But the trend for students to seek ways to test themselves in the real world, apart from low-paying student jobs, promises to continue for some time to come.

National Service

The push for some form of "national service" goes back to the Vietnam era when war protestors asked why military service was the only option for "serving" your country. In late 1990, the Bush Administration passed The National and Community Service (there's that term again!) Act. The Clinton Administration added money for summer and full-time service corps. In 1994, Congress merged a number of federal programs, including everything once under the umbrella of ACTION, into the "Corporation for National and Community Service."

Again, if you are unfamiliar with these developments— learn about them. For purposes of this book on recruitment, let's consider what impact this national and presidential attention to "service" may mean. First, rarely if ever does the federal initiative use the word "volunteer." This is because several of the key programs funded under the Act involve both a minimum wage "stipend" and an after-service cash benefit applicable to student loans. Your agency may be able to apply for an "AmeriCorps" participant (this is the overall name being used to describe the various full-time service corps being administered by the Corporation). But chances are that you will never even see an AmeriCorps worker. Only a few thousand citizens will be deployed under the program and we're a big country.

However, the political talk about community service may make the public more open to your volunteer recruiting pitch. People may be considering whether they can or should be more involved in community problem solving. In his inaugural address, President Clinton said: "There is nothing wrong with America that cannot be cured by what is right with America." Can you use that approach in your public speaking, too?

Otherwise, my sense is that this is a "trend" with little grassroots impact. If I'm wrong, *use* the impact to your advantage.

The Americans with Disabilities Act

Now it's the law. Any opportunity offered to

an able-bodied person must be made accessible to people with disabilities. Volunteer programs have long agreed that differently-able people can be wonderful contributors. Today, however, your organization must be prepared to adapt the physical environment for volunteers as well as for clients and employees.

The term "disabled" covers an enormous range of diagnoses—everything from physical to mental conditions, even being HIV-positive. Form linkages with organizations that serve various disability populations. Many are actively seeking ways for their members/clients to serve the community while gaining confidence or new skills.

One source of information about working with volunteers who are differently-abled is the booklet, "The Americans with Disabilities Act: Information and Implications for Volunteer Program Administrators," compiled by the Virginia Office of Volunteerism (1992).

The Changing Family

Divorce, single parenthood by choice, both partners in the paid workforce, blended step-families—I doubt that I have to explain what is happening to the concept of "family" in our society today. How does this impact on volunteering? Just a few effects:

- Stressed-out parents with less time to fill the traditional volunteer roles of Scout leader, PTA officer, homeroom aide.

- Fewer people at home during the day to help the school or youth group.

- A large number of non-custodial parents seeking new relationships with their children.

In each case, the challenge to you as a recruiter is to examine your assumptions. For example:

- Are parents the only source of prospective volunteers or can you find non-related adults more able to help children?

- Is there a way to recruit families *together* so that, instead of giving them one more rea-

son to be apart, the family can enjoy an activity as a unit?

- Can you "buddy up" volunteers so that two people can "job share" a responsibility and one can cover for the other if a particular week is hard?

- Can you recruit middle-aged divorced people by offering them a *social outlet* that is safer and more appealing than a singles bar?

- Can you consciously design work for a parent and child to do together and then recruit the noncustodial parent to team with his or her youngster on "visiting weekend"?

Nonsexist Roles

There was a time when men served on boards of directors and women did the hands-on volunteer work. As feminism raised everyone's consciousness, volunteering became more politically correct. Today, women are also tapped to be policy makers and men also serve in the trenches. But sex-typing continues in volunteer jobs as in the paid work force.

Analyze your volunteer placement patterns. Is there a reason why more male volunteers work in one unit than in another—or why they seem to be absent from some assignments? What about female volunteers? How can your recruitment efforts address such imbalance?

Aging of the Population

All demographers agree that people are living longer and healthier—and wait until the Baby Boomers turn sixty! We are pushing back the age of retirement and all our images of "old" are under question. This has great ramifications for volunteer recruitment. On one side of the scale, there is a large pool of younger seniors with skills, mobility, and time. On the other side, the fastest growing age category is ninety-plus and few organizations have perfected ways to tap this newest group of potential volunteers. There are contradictions, as well. For every person who takes early retirement at age fifty-five, there is a senior who continues to work at a paying job past age seventy.

What does the Census say about your community? What is the age spread today? Are you losing seniors to the Sun Belt? Are you *in* the Sun Belt and have a disproportionate number of older citizens?

For some organizations, the issue may be that volunteers are "aging in place." They joined you when they were middle aged and have remained loyal and active. But are their abilities changing? If you have not continued to recruit new, younger volunteers is it now hard to attract anyone other than another older volunteer?

For an excellent, in-depth study of why older people volunteer and how you can recruit and work with them, read *Older Volunteers: A Guide to Research and Practice* by Lucy Rose Fischer and Kay Banister Schaffer (Sage Publications, 1993).

Other Demographic Changes

I need only use the term "diversity" to elicit a response. Our North American society is shifting from a white, European majority to a more colorful and varied population. But the old goals of integration and assimilation are being challenged by newer goals of "together with diversity."

What is the racial and ethnic makeup of your community? Of your clients? Of your staff? Of the volunteers? What do you want it to be and what steps must you take to diversify the volunteer corps? We'll return to this subject in Chapter 11.

Transitional Volunteering

People undergo many changes as they age and as they cope with social stresses. In her book *Transitioning* (Vancouver Voluntary Action Resource Centre, 1981), Eva Schindler-Rainman identifies a long list of small and major transitions experienced by everyone at some point in life: births, deaths, graduations, marriages, moves, retirement, and so on. At each point of change, a person experiences different needs for community involvement. When we give people the chance to volunteer, we are tapping this life cycle of con-

nections, friendships, and self-esteem.

Some volunteer projects actively use formal transitions as the basis for volunteer work. For example, you can link with a corporation's pre-retirement counseling project to offer pending retirees a chance for a "second career." You can develop placements for patients completing a program of therapy so that they have a sheltered work experience as a stepping stone to a paid job.

Modern life requires the ability to deal with change, even chaos. Traditionally, volunteer projects have searched for people in a stable family or job situation and have considered people in transition as too uncertain to approach. The trend today is to recognize "transition" as a constant! And to welcome volunteers for what they can offer in the time they have.

The Economy

For some time now, North American society has been battling a changing economy. Whether or not you assess economic conditions as good or bad depends greatly on where you live and what job you hold. Some areas have been devastated by the loss of jobs, others have benefitted from new industries. It is generally acknowledged that the split between the have's and have-not's widens each year. A case can be made for serious pessimism but also for recovery.

Uninformed people think that volunteering lessens when economic times are hard. This thinking is based on the misconception that only people who are well-off can enjoy the luxury of volunteering. Experienced volunteer program managers can attest to the fact that hard times bring out the best in people. It is actually easier to recruit when social problems are self-evident. Even if people are suffering economically themselves, it is fulfilling to help others who may be worse off. Volunteering can also be a form of mutual aid, allowing all participants to benefit together. And volunteering is a way to help without necessarily having to give a financial donation.

If your area has a high rate of unemployment, consider how you might craft volunteer jobs to be a re-training opportunity. Can you offer your neighbors a way to improve their résumés, learn new and possibly employable skills, or at least keep their self-esteem while job hunting? Can you be flexible in scheduling so that someone can go to a job interview as often as necessary? If people are working two jobs to make ends meet, is there a way they can be a helpful volunteer even if they have less time to give than before?

Never assume that poverty deprives people of the desire to help others or that unemployed people do not have talents to share. Reach out and make volunteering a valuable exchange of needs and benefits.

Unemployment Compensation and Disability Leave Programs

In some states, people who are receiving unemployment or disability benefits are told that too many hours of volunteer work can jeopardize their status. (The theory being that if you can do that much volunteer work, maybe you are not looking hard enough for a new job or you are ready to go back to your regular job.) What is the law in your state or province? If it is restrictive, maybe you can work with your volunteerism colleagues to advocate for a more liberal ruling permitting increased volunteer activity.

In other areas, volunteer work is recognized as a legitimate way to maintain an active résumé or as a form of occupational or even physical therapy. In fact, a few employers (who foot the bill for unemployment and disability payments) have begun something new: *requiring* employees to do community service work while receiving the benefits! The twist in thinking here is that, if the company is paying for the employee to be out of work, why not "donate" some of that employee's time to the community? The same is true when companies pay severance after a plant closing.

This is yet another gray area of "mandated" volunteering, but if you know of a corporation that is instituting this type of policy, can your organization become a beneficiary of this new source of help?

Service Credits

Some communities have been experimenting with a plan that gives volunteers a tangible pay-

back called "service credits" or "service dollars." The idea is that a central coordinating agency (often the municipal government itself) maintains a record of the hours contributed by registered volunteers. At some point in the future, people who have "banked" volunteer hours in service to others can "draw" upon the system to obtain volunteer services for themselves.

This concept started from a positive and a negative philosophy. On the plus side, originators recognized that some people (often seniors) had too much pride to request public services, even those they were entitled to such as homebound meal delivery or transportation. By establishing a project whereby a person could first *give* something into the system, service credit programs enable people to *take* offered help with self-respect.

The negative attitude motivating some service dollar advocates is the belief that people just won't do anything without a reward—that it is necessary to offer a big carrot or there will not be any volunteers in the future.

As with so many things, the success of a service credit project is dependent on how well it is managed. The more local, the better. The more defined the project, the better. For instance: how long will "credits" be recorded and what happens if a participant moves out of the area? Will all types of volunteering be credited, or just some types? You can see the questions that can be raised.

As with all the trends we are discussing here, if this one intrigues you, do some more research and see if you can tap into it.

Changes in Available Schedules

While there are still lots of people available for volunteer work during the day, Mondays to Fridays, the pool of "traditional" daytime volunteers is shrinking. Most agencies maintain a weekday schedule that may, in fact, no longer be convenient for the *clients*, let alone for volunteers. We may well ask when service-providing agencies will have hours on Tuesday to Saturday, from noon to 8:00 p.m. But that's another book!

Volunteers today want flexibility in when they can contribute their time. Organizations that can accommodate volunteers in the evenings or on weekends will be rewarded with new recruits.

Similarly, changing perspectives on the work might result in some tasks being "exported"—can a volunteer do something at home or at work rather than on-site in your agency? Would a fax or computer modem allow electronic transfer of work between volunteers and the office (and each other)?

Short-term Assignments

For at least the past ten years, studies about who volunteers and why have verified what most directors of volunteers have learned in practice: many people prefer volunteer assignments that are results-oriented and short-term in nature. This should not be surprising. Employees rarely receive that gold watch after twenty-five years on the same job any more. So why should we expect volunteers to stick around forever?

Yet many organizations design volunteer roles with the assumption that volunteers will sign on for a long time. Some will. But it is more likely that today's volunteer will be interested in a *finite* assignment—one with a clear beginning, middle and end. The good news is that planning that type of volunteer work makes us more thoughtful about how we will use each volunteer's talents. Is there a goal or product? Why not?

Experience has shown that a percentage of volunteers who seek short-term assignments will "re-up" for a new assignment if the first one was satisfying. So you may end up with sequential, "episodic" commitments over a longer period of time. Nancy Macduff's book on *Episodic Volunteering* (MBA Publishing, 1991) examines this trend.

Corporate Volunteerism

The role of business in philanthropy and civic life is a continuing subject of discussion. One form of corporate social responsibility is the encouragement of employee volunteering. But this can range widely from simply letting employees know about volunteer work they can do on their own time to allowing employees company-paid "release time" to do community service during the work day. The volunteer field has seen a great deal of rhetoric about corporate volunteering, most of it about the

largest of companies. What is really happening in your local community? Do you know which companies have formal employee volunteer efforts? Which have "Dollars for Doers" programs that make a financial contribution to agencies in which employees volunteer their time? Are you tapping these?

We will spend more time on corporate volunteerism in Chapter 12. It is a trend that ebbs and flows, but today most business people acknowledge the need to get involved in community issues. This opens the door for you.

Trends and Issues in Your Field of Work

In addition to understanding the changes going on in volunteerism, you must also be aware of what may be evolving in your field of work. It is impossible to recruit volunteers to work in a hospital today without recognizing the impact of changes in health care, the politics of health care reform, the desperation of those without medical insurance, and other current issues. If you are recruiting for a library system, you may need to account for municipal budget cutbacks, the problem of adult illiteracy, or the growing number of non-English speaking people in certain neighborhoods.

You may want to survey others in your organization for their assessment of what trends are most affecting their work. Do some reading of the literature in your specialized field. Then consider how all of this can or should affect the way you recruit volunteers.

Trends and Issues That Seem Unrelated to Volunteering

This chapter has examined trends that can already be shown to affect volunteering. Who knows what might lurk around the corner? For example, the continuing AIDS epidemic will have implications for every work site and will therefore have an impact on volunteering even if your organization is not an AIDS services provider. Your client group—or volunteers—may be affected by AIDS, or volunteer screening procedures might need to be evaluated for compliance with diagnosis confidentiality.

A different example is the rapid revolution in office technology. Computers, faxes, modems—all are entering even the smallest work site and need constant upgrading. This trend not only affects the way we run the volunteer office and keep records on volunteer service, but also has the potential to create whole new types of volunteer assignments.

Some trends pose problems, others open new doors of possibility. Some begin as negative and surprise us by becoming positive—and vice versa. My goal here is to broaden your perspective on how your search for volunteers fits into the life of the community. Prospective recruits are dealing with many things: changes in their jobs, building a personal family life, finding ways to have some fun, keeping healthy. In addition to the private sphere, people do have an interest in the social welfare of their community. Your challenge is to inject your invitation to volunteer into the mix of things demanding people's time and attention. The more aware you are of what concerns your audience, the better able you will be to integrate volunteering into people's lifestyles. To end this chapter as it began: volunteering does not occur in a vacuum.

Where to Look for Volunteers

The ability to identify *where* to find prospective volunteers is at the heart of successful recruitment. If the right people hear your message, you have a good chance of motivating candidates. But if you are trying to "sell" to the wrong audience, you won't end up with recruits. This is classic marketing common sense. We are talking about "targeting" the segment of the community or population that you most hope to attract as volunteers.

Recognize that this part of the process takes place at your desk, *before* you do any other recruitment task—particularly before you spend any time or money on recruitment materials. Because it is so important to do this thinking about the potential sources of volunteers creatively and well, you might want to ask a few people to spend an afternoon as a "Recruitment Think Tank" with you every six months or so. The synergy of several minds at work will produce a much more innovative list of options—and you'll enjoy the process more, too.

Keep in mind:

There are no rules for where you can (or cannot) recruit!

In fact, the volunteer community has been singularly uncreative in finding places in which to encourage people to volunteer. Recruiters tend to go to the same sources over and over again, often in direct competition with lots of other organizations trying to recruit volunteers from the same site. If you can identify new places to look, your whole approach will be fresher . . . and ultimately more successful.

The Process of Identifying Sources

Concentrate on *one* volunteer job description at a time. The logic of this important recommendation should be clear: the places where you might find an arts and crafts instructor will not be the same as those where you might find a crisis hot line worker . . . so why try to recruit them at the same time? You (and your Recruitment Think Tank) should ask:

"Where in our community might we find people who have the skills (or background, or characteristics) this volunteer job description requires?"

This question is deceptively simple looking. In answering it, you must keep yourself *focused*. Otherwise, you will soon find yourself wandering off on the tangent that really deals with "where can we find *people* (in general)?"

Let's look at an example. Let's say you need a volunteer who can do calligraphy. By asking: "Where can we find someone who is skilled at calligraphy?" you might brainstorm a list like this:

- Art classes studying pen and ink
- Businesses that specialize in producing invitations
- Graphics departments of major corporations

- Local freelance artists association
- Japanese art society
- Large catering firms that also do invitations
- Companies with computers that do calligraphy
- Sign-making companies
- Art supply stores that sell calligraphy pens and inks

As you can see, each of these sources has a better-than-equal chance for you to locate someone there who does calligraphy. And once you know you are in contact with the right prospects, *then* you can try to recruit them.

Note that the above list does *not* include general public places such as "churches" or "schools." These are not sufficiently specific—you cannot be certain that you will find anyone with the skill you seek and therefore will be wasting time and effort sending your message to people who probably cannot help you.

Do not let yourself subconsciously "edit" the list while you are brainstorming. For example, it is easy to dismiss an idea without listing it just because you aren't sure how to locate the source or perhaps don't know *how* to do recruitment there. Those questions come later in the process. Right now your challenge is simply to answer the question: "Where might we *find* X?"

Let's look at another example. Say you need automobile drivers for a variety of escort and delivery routes. Again, the question for brainstorming is: "Where in our community can we find people who drive cars?" Avoid the general response of thinking, "why, everywhere!" Consider the following *specific* ideas:

- car washes
- Traffic Court
- the Motor Vehicle Bureau
- drivers' education classes
- drive-in windows
- gas stations
- car showrooms
- taxi and bus depots
- truck stops
- drive-in movies

- car repair shops
- car accessory stores
- parking lots
- tire and auto parts stores
- car rallies
- car shows

When you saw "Traffic Court" as the second response, did you react negatively? Remember that this is not yet a list of definite sources of *volunteers*. It is a list of places where we can find *drivers*.

Now you have to go to step two: editing. If you are looking for volunteers to drive *people*, you may well want to delete Traffic Court from further consideration. But if the volunteers will be driving *things* (maybe delivering holiday baskets, for example), then Traffic Court might be a great idea. In a small community, especially, the judge might welcome an alternative sentencing option for first offenders or for those unable to pay a fine. And you may have found a great source of help.

So, in the editing stage you:

1. Delete any ideas that do not seem feasible (but allow some discussion so that an idea is not dismissed simply because it is unusual).

2. Prioritize the list in order of which seem the most likely sources of prospects down to the least likely.

3. Localize the list: exactly *which* companies, stores, or organizations in your town or neighborhood match this idea? You may need to do some research as to what is available, at least with the Yellow Pages of the telephone book.

4. As you identify real places, put these into priority order, too. Some criteria are:

   —Which are geographically close to you?

   —Which are already linked to you in some way? For instance, which might be donors or participants in a collaborative effort?

   —Does anyone in your organization have an inside contact at any of the sources, such as a spouse or friend who works there?

   —Is this source appealing to you for some reason? (Yes, this is a valid criterion. If you *enjoy* the tasks of recruitment, you will be more enthusiastic at it. So go ahead and select sources that sound like fun to contact.)

All of the above would be good reasons to move a potential source higher up on the list.

5. If you are particularly interested in recruiting a certain racial or ethnic group, focus your identification further. Such as: which of the stores is in a Spanish-speaking neighborhood? The same holds true for sex and age diversity. Which organization has a predominantly male membership? Which shop holds special sales for senior citizens? (More on diversity in Chapter 11 and on special target audiences in Chapter 12.)

Going back to the brainstormed list for drivers, you might eliminate such sources as truck stops or gas stations because too many of the patrons would be transients who do not live in your town. You might spend more time analyzing the drive-in window idea and consider working with neighborhood banks that have drive-in windows because you can select several banks in different parts of town. Or you might remember that every April there is a big car rally at the park and you never thought about using that event for your volunteer recruitment goals.

You can see how this process lets you discover possible sources for help that you might not otherwise have considered. It certainly forces you to go beyond the "traditional" places to look for volunteers. And it can insure that you do not go to the wrong places to recruit—if you are not communicating with the right target audience for your needs, you are wasting your time.

The above discussion should also make it clear why you must start with sources before selecting a recruitment "technique." Some of the sources do not lend themselves to any of the techniques we will discuss in the next chapter. The only way to tap such sites is to adapt to their special situations or to work with someone there. If you want to recruit at the neighborhood library, you are unlikely to use your new music video there! A corporation might let you talk to department heads or might suggest that you set up a table in the employee cafeteria.

Characteristics as Well as Skills

This brainstorming of "where can we find people with the skills we need" can also work for other characteristics. For example, one of the concerns of the volunteer world is that daytime volunteers are an endangered species. In the past, organizations grew complacent in their dependency on female homemakers. When women took paying jobs (though in fact some female full-time homemakers still exist), such agencies found themselves without their accustomed source of volunteers. If you are in this situation, your brainstorming question may have to be: "where can we find people who are available Monday to Friday, 9:00 a.m. to 5:00 p.m.?"

You will find your responses centering around the large segment of the workforce who do not work "normal" hours. In fact, logic shows that "normal" hours are relative indeed. Think about all the jobs that require: shift work; predominantly evening hours; weekend days; or odd or flexible schedules.

Shift Work: A wide variety of institutions and businesses function twenty-four hours a day or at least on double shift. This means that many people who work 7:00 a.m. to 3:00 p.m. or 3:00 to 11:00 p.m. have discretionary time available overlapping the 9:00 to 5:00 agency day. Even the night shift might be attracted to early morning volunteer work. If you select worksites close to your organization's location, one of your recruitment pitches can be: "help us out on your way to or from work with very little extra commuting."

Consider the range of people and skills available in 24-hour worksites: hospitals and residential treatment programs; many factories; television and radio stations; police and fire departments; telephone companies; hotels; the military; the Postal Service and overnight delivery companies.

Evening Workers: In the same vein, identify businesses employing people mainly in the evening hours. Such workers often sleep late after a long night at work, but are prospective volunteers in the afternoon. Some sites are: restaurants; theaters; newspapers; astronomy labs; janitorial services; computer services.

Weekend Workers: Quite a number of jobs require Saturday and/or Sunday shifts, thereby giving employees a full day or two off during the week: parks and recreation programs; most cultural attractions such as museums and historic sites; churches and synagogues; libraries; shopping malls; hair salons; sports and country clubs. Some jobs overlap categories, especially retail sales which employ people on the weekends and in the evenings.

Odd or "Free-to-Choose" Schedules: Some employed people work on changing, inconsistent, or temporary schedules. While this may make it difficult to place such volunteers in regular assignments, they are nevertheless excellent resources for volunteering that focuses on producing a result rather than requiring a specific time commitment. Consider: airline personnel; substitute teachers; "temps" of all sorts; long distance truck drivers; farmers; university faculty; collection agents.

The Self-Employed: A whole sub-category involves people who are self-employed or work on commission. They can choose to volunteer during a weekday and "make up" the work time later. For example: consultants; artists; anyone who works at home; sole practitioners in fields such as accounting or public relations; real estate agents.

It is probably worthwhile to point out that the higher a person rises in a company, the more flexibility s/he has in allocating his or her schedule. So you can consider top executives more likely weekday recruits than secretaries who have less choice about how to use their workday time.

By focusing your brainstorming session only on the daytime availability question, you can see how wide a range of options you can generate. Now you can take this set of ideas and narrow it further by considering which of these sources might provide the skills you need.

Rural Communities

It is at this point that our colleagues in rural communities sigh deeply. They feel that any discussion of sources of volunteers has an urban or suburban slant—larger populations mean more places to look for volunteers. Conversely, they feel that rural areas have fewer resources to tap. Let's examine this more closely.

First, while there are fewer prospective volunteers in rural communities, there are also fewer clients. The number of volunteers needed is usually in proportion to the numbers of people served. Most rural agencies would be overwhelmed by the scope of what is commonplace in New York City, where quite a number of agencies routinely involve between 500 and 3,000 volunteers each month. So it may be a challenge to find the right volunteers in a rural area, but you probably are only looking for a limited number of candidates at any given time.

The process of brainstorming that we have been discussing here works equally well for rural areas, even if the list you generate is shorter than it might be in a more populated township. Never assume that you are working in a community with no resources, no matter how small. A number of years ago *The Journal of Volunteer Administration* published a fascinating article about the experiences of the Office of Aging in Fayette County, Pennsylvania.[1] Fayette County, in the far southwest corner of Pennsylvania, is considered part of Appalachia and has a rural, aging, and poor population. The AAA wanted to recruit volunteers to work with frail, homebound elderly clients and obtained a grant to study the feasibility of this idea. Starting from the (untested) proposition that individual volunteers would be hard to find, the AAA wanted to work with established civic groups to see if they could be enticed to "adopt" a senior. The first part of the study, therefore, was to identify what membership associations existed in the county.

The researchers stopped counting at 319 groups! They were completely amazed to discover that this "have-not" county, so often described as having no resources, in fact had an abundance of organizations! Until this study, however, these groups had been invisible as a resource. The study uncovered civic clubs such as the Kiwanis, religious groups such as the Knights of Columbus and Lutheran Church Women, hobby clubs such as gardeners and stamp collectors, recreation groups such as bowling leagues, and youth groups such as 4-H. The study proved the continuing validity of de Tocqueville's observation of America as a country of "joiners." In fact, the case could be made that the need for people to interact in groups may be stronger in a rural area than in an urban neighborhood because local residents understand the need to combat isolation.

Apart from the proliferation of associations, rural communities have clear centers of activity. Yes, there may only be one high school, but that means that you can learn how that institution works: who has influence, which teachers encourage service-learning (and who may never have been asked to help), which student clubs are the most active. You can also identify the place most residents come to buy their groceries or picnic on a summer afternoon. Your challenge, therefore, may be less where to look than how to communicate your message.

Urban Settings

As someone who has always lived and worked in cities, I feel the need to add that the urban recruiter who sees the whole city as one big pool of volunteer talent is headed for disappointment. In truth, cities are a collection of neighborhoods as different from one another as are rural "hollers." The ethnic make-up of each neighborhood is only one difference. Each will have a distinct culture, center of activity, and influential leaders. Whether you are recruiting in an urban, suburban, or rural community, the best advice is always to do your homework. The more informed you are about the way people interact in a given locality, the more likely you will find the best ways to send your recruitment message.

Piggybacking

The brainstormed idea on page 47 about using the annual car rally to your own ends leads into a guiding principle for recruitment: "piggyback" whenever you can. If someone else has done all the work of bringing a lot of people out for an event, why not make use of that opportunity? And the fun part is that—if you choose your piggybacking options wisely —the initiating group will be *happy* you are participating.

The car rally, generally a purely recreational

or even profit-making event, might be delighted at the chance to show community or charitable spirit by giving you a booth or letting you advertise in their program. It may never have occurred to them that their audience of car lovers might be of potential interest to a volunteer recruiter.

Another type of piggybacking is to link volunteer recruitment with holiday events. Thanksgiving is a great time to say "thanks" to volunteers and remind others of ways to give. Labor Day can be used to turn attention to unpaid as well as paid workers. Even if your organization does not schedule a volunteer recognition event during National Volunteer Week (usually the third week of April each year), ride on the coat tails of any national or local publicity generated to draw attention to volunteering with you. Be the first to let your community know that December 5 (in some years, December 6) is International Volunteer Day, as declared by the United Nations and celebrated in a number of countries around the world.

It is possible to piggyback on your own organization's events. When you begin to think in these terms, you will see that you may have had many *missed opportunities*! Does your agency sponsor any annual fundraisers, open houses, or workshops? If so, make certain you have a visible display booth or program ad describing volunteer opportunities. For that matter, are you making full use of your facilities' bulletin boards and hallways? Are volunteer opportunities included in the new client packet? Mentioned in client exit interviews? You get the point.

Finally, don't overlook the value of the annual volunteer recognition event to spread the word about new volunteer positions while you are thanking people for last year's efforts.

Your "Circle of Resources"

One of my favorite suggestions for volunteer recruitment is also one of the simplest: start with the resources in closest proximity to your agency. What untapped treasures might be across the street or on the next block?

Picture your facility as the center of a bull's eye, with concentric circles around it. Now do the following. If you are in an urban area, walk out your front door with a clipboard and pen (take along a volunteer for company). If you are more rural, do this by driving. The point is to walk completely around the block (or drive in a tight circle) and *write down everything you see:* stores, businesses, parking lots, churches, apartment houses, schools, etc. A "Proximity Chart" worksheet for your use is on the next page.

It is vital to actually do this action physically, even if you feel reasonably sure that you know what is in your neighborhood. Why? Because you will soon discover that: 1) you tend to be aware only of the things that are present in the one direction that you take to work every day; 2) after a while you no longer see what you are looking at; and 3) some of the things you see may not be identifiable. An example of this last point is passing a company with the name "Mighty Corporation" emblazoned on a large sign. Do you know from that name what work this company does? Probably not.

After you have inventoried everything on your street, the two side streets, and the street in back of you, move on to a two-block radius and do the same. As time permits, keep going in widening concentric circles. If you are driving, keep taking right (or left!) turns and inventory a quarter-mile radius, then a half-mile radius, etc. Note that if your offices are in a high-rise building, your first task is to take the elevator to each floor and see who your neighbors are above and below you.

You may be skeptical about this recommendation, but I assure you that you will find a number of "neighbors" that you did not know you had. And this means potential resources.

Now that you have your list, analyze it. If there are mysteries such as "Mighty Corporation," find out what happens there. Your goal is to identify any number of ways your neighbors might help you to accomplish your goals:

- Might there be business people who could volunteer at your site on their way to or from work, or even at lunchtime? Might there be students or seniors with daytime hours available? Might any of your neighbors have an interest in community service projects of any sort?

- What professional skills might be tapped at neighboring businesses or schools? (Be sure to watch for sole practitioners such as art-

ists, consultants, accountants, and others with valuable talents—and who control their own work schedules.)

- Might there be access to other types of resources beyond volunteers: donated goods or materials, storage space, parking space, use of various loaned equipment, etc.?

- Do any of these neighbors share your service goals, an interest in your client population, or have anything else in common with you that might lead to collaboration of some sort?

Making contact with your neighbors is much easier than approaching resources across town. After all, it is always legitimate to make the acquaintance of folks nearby. Develop a special flyer or letter introducing your agency and address it to: "Our neighbors." Explain the services you offer (include a brochure if you have one) and, if appropriate, welcome visitors. Depending on your comfort level and on the culture of your neighborhood, mail the materials in small batches and follow up within a week by phone, or go in person to deliver the material.

Do not feel that these are "cold calls." As a representative of your organization, you want to spread the word about the good work that you do. It will be of benefit to your neighbors to be better informed about an agency in such close proximity. And, for both sides, there is great potential to share resources. Your opening line is: "Hi. Do you realize that we can see your top floor from our backyard?" Or some variation on that theme.

Express as much genuine interest in your neighbors as you wish them to show in you. Ask questions about their work and constituents. Perhaps there is some help that you can offer to them. Maybe a collaborative effort can help everyone. Is there something you can barter or exchange? What goes around, comes around. When you demonstrate good neighborliness, it sets the tone for future relationships.

You have several goals for these contacts. First, you want your neighbors to be informed about your agency. They can help with everything from security to giving directions to lost clients. Second, some of your neighbors may actually need your services for themselves or their contacts, so

Proximity Chart

3

2

1

STARTING ADDRESS

	HAS POTENTIAL	NEED MORE INFO

ZONE 2 (Surrounding Blocks or Half Mile)

	HAS POTENTIAL	NEED MORE INFO

ZONE 1 (1 Block or Quarter Mile)

Name and Address	HAS POTENTIAL	NEED MORE INFO			

Continue as far as your legs (or vehicle)
will carry you.

this is a form of client development. Third, such outreach is positive public relations; you never know when a zoning issue or other concern will require the support of those who live in your area.

Finally, once you have established communication, you can explain your search for active volunteers (or for whatever other resources you hope to get from each site). The volunteers might be your neighbors themselves or their friends and customers who regularly come to your neighborhood. Note that all of these possible goals hold true even if your closest "neighbor" is a mile away.

You may be successful at once. More likely, you will be sowing recruitment seeds. Perhaps you can leave some flyers in the doctor's waiting room or on the community center bulletin board. Maybe you can arrange to speak at the fall tenant council meeting.

What are some actual examples of resource finding that resulted from this approach? After struggling to reimburse rising expenses, a women's crisis center obtained two free parking spaces for volunteer counselors in the private parking garage of a corporate headquarters building across the street from the center. Simply by taking the time to introduce themselves to everyone on their block, a delinquency prevention program was offered free, day-old baked goods from a wholesale bakery neighbor (provided the program sent someone to pick up the goodies every day). A senior center was invited to join the annual block party for the first time, providing the opportunity for social interaction on both sides.

What might *you* find? Whether you are located in the heart of downtown or miles from anywhere, you have neighbors. Because all sorts of people and businesses volunteer their time and resources to a myriad of causes, everyone is a potential source of help. Sharing a location starts you off with something in common. It's hard to find a better recruiting pitch.

One More Proximity Idea

This proximity approach can work in other ways, too. If you are recruiting volunteers to do friendly visiting or deliver homebound meals, try putting the *client's address* in the center of the bull's eye. For coaching or tutoring, use the play-ing field or the library branch where the lessons will be given as the location in the center. Then identify the "circle of resources" around that site.

Remember that it is a powerful motivator to be able to say: "you can be of help to someone just around the corner." It is overwhelming to hear about sixty seniors who need meal delivery in the two-county area, but it is manageable to consider serving the one older person in this very neighborhood.

Spheres of Influence

Another approach to sources of potential volunteers uses a variation on the concentric circles theme. This involves evaluating and diagnosing who your organization "touches" in the course of a year . . . yet who may never have been considered (or even considered themselves) a volunteer resource. You can create a "map" of how your "spheres of influence" overlap and connect.

The best way to explain this concept is to discuss two actual examples of spheres of influence maps that I helped two very different clients create as part of their recruitment strategies.

Youth for Understanding (YFU) places international students in private homes with American host families and also sends American students abroad for a similar experience. We considered the following questions together and came up with these answers:

1. *Who comes in contact with the foreign students while they are in the United States?*

   Answers:
   —the people at the schools they attend: not just the immediate teachers and classmates, but the whole school . . . meaning lots more teachers and lots more schoolmates (. . . and *their* families, etc.)
   —participants in social activities in which the student engages
   —American relatives of the students or family friends

2. *Who comes in contact with host families while the foreign students are in their homes?*
   Answers:
   —relatives, extended family

—neighbors
—friends
—places of employment for the host parents
—the civic organizations to which the host family belongs
—the family's place of worship

3. *Who is aware of American students who go abroad with YFU?*

   Answers:
   —the students' families and friends
   —the students' schools
   —anyone listening to the parents talking about their child being overseas: fellow employees, civic club members, etc.

4. *Who else has a stake in the work of YFU?*

   Answers:
   —American "alumni" of the overseas experience
   —past host families
   —donors
   —current volunteers in other roles
   —other organizations with a mission to insure foreign exchange, international education, etc.

Using the answers to these questions we "mapped" YFU's spheres of influence (see next page), showing the overlapping circles of contacts, moving from people clearly involved with YFU to those peripherally interested. By the time we had identified this large constellation of people, it was clear that the organization had not even begun to tap the potential "market" of people *already aware* of the work of the group! Yet time and effort had been expended reaching out to the *general public* (often uninformed about YFU) before "starting at home."

The second example involves a predominantly volunteer organization (only a few paid staff and many volunteer members) who are working to combat a fatal disease. Traditionally, this organization provided services to families at a time of crisis and was reluctant to be perceived as "recruiting" the people they felt were recipients of service. However, once time had passed after the death of the loved one, the organization "hoped" that people would want to become involved in helping others. (In point of fact, few people were

actually directly asked to do so, even after time had passed.)

If they wanted to increase their volunteer recruitment success, we talked about needing a major change of mindset: accepting that there are more people to reach out to than the immediate family. In fact, some of the people we identified as prospective volunteers might actually *welcome* an immediate recruitment effort as an outlet for their concern about the problem.

For this organization, we mapped their spheres of influence by answering the following questions:

1. *Who else is deeply affected by this fatal illness, other than the nuclear family?*

   Answers:
   —the grandparents, uncles, aunts, and other extended family members
   —good friends of the family
   —colleagues at work
   —neighbors
   —members of the religious congregation in which the family worships

2. *Who else is aware of this problem, but perhaps without the personal emotional ties to an individual death?*

   Answers:
   —doctors and nurses who treat the patients
   —clergy and other counselors
   —funeral directors
   —donors

The first category represents people with a personal stake in curing the disease. They, in turn, can be subdivided into all sorts of skills, professions, and backgrounds. The second group is already "trained" in certain fields. How might they be used to do the work of the organization?

These examples should illustrate how this type of mapping exercise can make formerly invisible sources visible. Again, use your Recruitment Think Tank to map your organization's spheres of influence. Have you been missing opportunities to spread the word about volunteer roles? Are there "hot prospects" waiting to hear from you? A few possibilities include past satisfied clients or their families, people who come to your annual special events, or financial donors (who may never have

Spheres of Influence in YFU

This page (provided courtesy of Youth for Understanding, Washington, DC) shows how Youth for Understanding developed its spheres of influence "map" after our training session identified its potential audiences (see page 52). Don't worry about understanding all of YFU's abbreviations or contact groups. Instead, see how the map shows the interrelationships, overlaps, and connections among YFU's various audiences. Primary recruitment prospects are those closest on the map to the International Students and Host Families or to the Americans Overseas participants. As the circles expand outward, the potential target audiences have more distant contact programmatically and geographically.

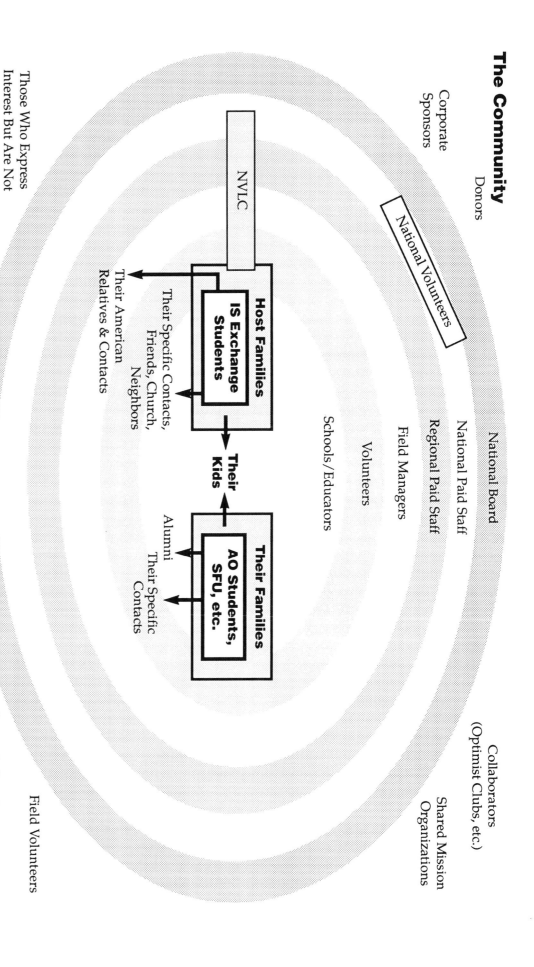

The Community
Donors

Corporate
Sponsors

National Volunteers

National Board

National Paid Staff

Regional Paid Staff

Field Managers

Volunteers

Schools/Educators

NVLC

Host Families
IS Exchange Students

Their American
Relatives & Contacts

Their Specific Contacts,
Friends, Church,
Neighbors

Their Kids

Their Families
AO Students, SFU, etc.

Alumni
Their Specific
Contacts

Collaborators
(Optimist Clubs, etc.)

Shared Mission
Organizations

Those Who Express
Interest But Are Not
Followed Up

Currently Inactive
The Community

Field Volunteers

been asked to give their time as well as their money).

In all cases:

Just because people know what you do, never assume they know that they can become involved as volunteers! Nor that you need *them*!

They have to be *asked*.

Going Beyond Your Spheres

Having just exhorted you to begin recruiting from your inner circles first, let me also offer the opposite advice if it is applicable. Some organizations assume that people will not volunteer for them if those people have no previous contact with the organization's services. For instance, cultural and performing arts groups expect their audience, subscribers, or visitors to be the most likely source of volunteers. For the most part, this is an appropriate assumption. However, cultural groups also have the challenge of expanding their *audiences*. So outreach to new populations is important for several reasons.

People can be asked to volunteer for an organization because their skills are needed for a particular volunteer assignment. If the *task* interests the candidate, s/he may well agree to volunteer and thereby be *introduced* to the cultural arts group (perhaps eventually also joining its regular audience, though that should not be a requirement to volunteer). So go ahead and follow the guidelines already suggested for brainstorming to consider new sources of volunteers. *Start* with your spheres of influence, but don't stop there.

A Word about Finding Board Members and Fundraising Volunteers

The steps to successful recruitment of volunteers hold true for any type of volunteer sought, including new members of the board of directors, advisory council members, and volunteers to conduct fundraising efforts. However, in many agencies these groups of volunteers are managerially

separated from the direct-service "volunteer program." This is not the forum for discussing the pros and cons of such a division, but it is true that executive directors and development officers may be conducting their own recruitment campaigns alongside the efforts of the director of volunteers. If this is happening in your organization, call a summit meeting! Try to mesh and coordinate your recruiting attempts so that you help one another. After all, some of the people who initially are attracted to frontline volunteer work might be excellent candidates for the board (if not right away, then after some experience with your agency). Conversely, the people "rejected" as not right for the board or fundraising may actually be wonderful prospects for direct-service volunteering.

You are all in the business of winning friends for your organization. Assessing and deploying the talents of supporters should therefore be a shared priority. Valid issues of status may dictate who recruits board members, but the *planning* of outreach strategies can be a mutual responsibility.

There is another reason why it is important to connect board development with other volunteer recruitment: it is unrealistic to expect people to join you "at the top" if they have had no prior involvement with your organization.

It is a serious legal and fiduciary responsibility to be on a board of directors. While some civic leaders collect board memberships as a trophy list, you want board members who give you the time and energy the organization deserves. How can someone agree to such a heavy commitment without knowing you first? Potential board members might be recruited for board *committees* as a "practice run"—the committee term is a volunteer commitment unto itself, but both sides understand that it is a get-acquainted period to assess if a board appointment is a good idea. Or a potential board member might be recruited for any responsible frontline volunteer position. What could be a better orientation to the needs of the agency?

There is a growing body of literature about working with boards of directors, including how to recruit them. One valuable booklet is *How to Recruit Great Board Members* by Dorian Dodson (Adolfo Street Publications, 1993).

In a similar vein, how can you expect someone to raise money for you if they have not yet developed a personal commitment to the organization? The best fundraising evolves from the sincerity of the volunteers who become donors themselves and then ask others to donate, too. Build loyalty through direct service volunteer work and volunteers might even surprise themselves at their willingness to raise funds.

The development office might consider tying a fundraising campaign to offering opportunities to volunteer. Studies show that people who volunteer give a greater percentage of their income to charity than non-volunteers. There's a lesson to be learned in there somewhere.

Volunteer Referral Services

As you assess the resources in your community, you will become aware of a number of organizations whose mission it is to help people find good volunteer opportunities. Be sure that you register your organization with any clearinghouse, databank, directory or program offering volunteer referral services.

More than 400 communities in the United States and Canada have a Volunteer Center to help organizations and prospective volunteers find each other. Volunteer Centers may be called by names such as Voluntary Action Center, Volunteer Bureau (especially in Canada), or Volunteer Placement Service. Some are independent agencies, but many are part of the local United Way. There is also wide variation in the types of services Volunteer Centers provide, but the basic ones are:

- Volunteer Centers collect information from agencies and organizations about their volunteer needs. They then maintain databases, often on computer, so that prospective volunteers can identify possible placement sites. This "clearinghouse" function can include publishing various directories or lists of volunteer opportunities.

- Volunteer Centers will help individuals and groups seeking volunteer work by offering them the use of their databases on volunteer opportunities, talking to them about what is happening in a particular community, and sometimes conducting an initial personal interview as a first step in placement. They

may sponsor "volunteer fairs" at shopping malls or places of business, bringing together displays and representatives of agencies seeking volunteers so that the public becomes aware of the opportunities.

- Volunteer Centers coordinate annual "thank you" events to recognize the efforts of community volunteers. In the United States, this is often done in April, during National Volunteer Week (when much national and local publicity is generated about volunteers, starting with a Presidential proclamation). Canadian Volunteer Bureaus use the same model.

- Volunteer Centers provide training and consultation to leaders of volunteers in how to work effectively with their non-paid staffs. This can include workshops and conferences as well as on-site technical assistance.

Apart from these basic, core services, Volunteer Centers do many other things depending on the needs of their community. They may organize holiday toy drives, place court-referred volunteers, run special projects for students or seniors, or provide the local newspaper with a weekly column of volunteer opportunities.

Volunteer Centers are listed in the telephone book. Try any of the name variations above. Volunteer Centers may be found through their sponsoring agency if they are a division of a larger group. The most common sponsor is the United Way, so try your local United Way if you do not find a telephone listing for a separate Volunteer Center. Other sponsors may be the American Red Cross, the Junior League, or your municipal government. A growing number of Volunteer Centers are run by the Mayor's Office or as part of county government.

You can see why it is useful to be registered with your Volunteer Center.

Other Placement Services

A number of programs have been established specifically to help senior citizens find ways to remain active in their communities. The most widespread is the Retired and Senior Volunteer

Program, known as RSVP. Although RSVP is not a full Volunteer Center, its purpose is to help older Americans find meaningful volunteer work. An added benefit is that volunteers placed through RSVP receive some travel reimbursement and insurance. RSVP now works with people age fifty-five and older.

The American Association of Retired People (AARP) also has local chapters throughout the country and sponsors a Talent Bank program. SCORE, the Senior Corps of Retired Executives, helps the Small Business Administration to consult with emerging businesses, but it might be a source of help to a nonprofit as well.

More and more colleges and universities are establishing offices to link students with volunteer opportunities or "community service" placements. There are no standard names or locations of such offices, but any campus student activities staff should be able to direct you to their school's program if one exists. National and state "Campus Compact" organizations also publish lists of participating schools.

Student community service is extending to the high school level and even younger. Contact your local public school system to see who is coordinating student volunteer efforts and get your name on that person's referral list. Don't over look private and parochial schools, many of whom have been engaged in community service long before it came into vogue in the 1990's.

Some corporations have organized employee volunteer programs and allow agencies to register available volunteer positions. Think about civic organizations that regularly sponsor service projects. Make sure that they all know about your agency for the next round of planning.

It rarely costs anything to be on these types of lists and there are excellent public relations benefits from becoming known as an organization that wants help from volunteers. Periodically send updates of your openings for volunteers, even if you have not received a referral recently from a particular registry. These contacts may not offer immediate results and do not substitute for an active volunteer recruitment campaign of your own. But over time you will get referrals of prospective volunteers—often at the most unexpected, but always welcome, time.

If You Need an Army

The strategies in this chapter are based on the assumption that you have several volunteer job descriptions which you need to fill with a manageable number of volunteers—perhaps even only one person for each role. But you may be looking for a very large number of people for service at a special event. Where can you look for hundreds of people, all available on the same date, for tasks that require mainly energy and "turning up"?

If you approach such mass recruitment all at once, it will indeed be overwhelming. Instead, use the same approach as I have been recommending for filling any volunteer vacancy: break the search down into mini-campaigns, targeting prospective volunteers in logical ways.

First define the work to be done as specifically as possible. Is it really all the same or are some tasks clearly more specialized? For example, while most volunteers will staff exhibit booths, take tickets, etc., you may need about twenty people with money-handling and accounting skills. If so, then one of your mini-campaigns will be aimed at the financial/accounting community. The more you can identify such sub-groups within your mass of "volunteers needed," the more successful you will be in targeting the best sources of prospective volunteers.

For the remaining general tasks, find a different way of making the search more manageable. Divide your attention in ways such as:

- Groups having some connection to your organization (spheres of influence) or to the theme of the event.
- People from different geographic locations.
- People available mornings, or afternoons, or evenings.
- Different age categories.

If you need hundreds of volunteers, I hope that you are not alone in doing the recruitment! Assign each member of your recruiting team to a different target audience as suggested above and *focus* (there's that word again!) on where to find such prospects and how to attract them—just as with any smaller number of needed volunteers.

If You Are a Volunteer Center

The advice that I've just given to people who need to recruit large numbers of volunteers for one organization is equally pertinent to Volunteer Centers, RSVP, and other volunteer referral services seeking many volunteers for many placement sites. Your major ongoing challenge is to maintain the visibility of volunteerism *in general*. This will help each of your community agencies to be more successful in recruiting, as well. But if you are determined to find potential volunteer applicants, break the task down into mini-campaigns with targeted audiences, just as we have been discussing throughout this chapter.

Know Your Community

As a volunteer recruiter, you must study and know your community. What's out there? Rather than going back to the same small circle of resources over and over again, reach out to new places. Read the newspaper to learn about civic clubs or school projects. Be aware of new companies moving in. You might even want to join your local Chamber of Commerce to stay in the loop of current information.

It may be helpful to study the Census information for your area. Are there patterns of population shift? Are there growing numbers of people over age sixty or is this age group moving out of the county? What is the median income level? educational level?

Are there factors unique to your community? For example, if you are located in a vacation destination spot you may have out-of-town visitors year round or an influx at certain seasons. If va-cationers stay for several months, they may become a volunteer resource. Conversely, in the off season, the hotel staff might become a potential talent pool for you. The same type of analysis might work if you are in a college town, are affected by agricultural harvest times, or are the site for an annual folk festival.

Key Principles

Here are some of the guiding principles highlighted in this chapter:

- Success in recruitment rests with creative thinking about where to look for volunteers.
- Focus on each job description separately and use logic to find connections between your volunteer needs and what is available at a potential source.
- There are no rules. Just because no one else has tried to recruit at a certain site does not mean you can't be successful there.
- Start with the sources that attract you. If you feel comfortable making your recruitment appeal, you will be more effective than if you force yourself to contact a source that you feel you "should."

In Section III, you will find a chapter on "Appealing to Special Target Audiences." First you must do the creative thinking explained in this chapter in order to identify which target audiences might be best for you to approach. Chapter 12 then gives you a potpourri of tips and pointers to help you find these groups and make the "asking" more effective.

---

[1]Christine L. Young, PHD, Pamela J. Larson, MRP, and Donald Goughler, "Organizations as Volunteers for the Rural Frail Elderly," *The Journal of Volunteer Administration*, II, 1 (Fall 1983), pp. 33-44.

Since the 1994 original edition, the Internet has become a major tool for recruiters. For 21st century ideas, see the Appendix on "Outreach in Cyberspace" beginning on page 143.

SECTION II:

INVITATION

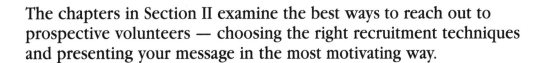

The chapters in Section II examine the best ways to reach out to prospective volunteers — choosing the right recruitment techniques and presenting your message in the most motivating way.

Techniques of Recruitment (Part One)

Now that we have identified all sorts of new places to look for volunteers, we are ready to figure out the best ways to do the asking. There are no perfect, right or wrong ways to recruit, but the most important thing is to *match the technique to the source*.

In this chapter we will examine common and less common techniques of volunteer recruitment—everything except printed materials. In the next chapter we'll look more carefully at the range of options you have for printing recruitment tools. In Chapter 9, we will consider the various ways you can word and present your recruitment information.

For all the techniques, I'll give some pros and cons for you to appraise. But remember—every recruiter has different experiences. While one person might swear by college bulletin boards, another recruiter might swear at them! If you have developed a logical strategy for tapping a source of prospective volunteers, give it a try. Similarly, even if someone else in your agency has been unsuccessful with a technique in the past, be willing to try it again if the situation has changed or if you think you have added a new twist.

Some recruitment efforts elicit immediate reaction from volunteer applicants. But don't be daunted by initial lack of response. Recruiting volunteers is a process of "sowing seeds." Give your outreach efforts a chance to take hold and seep through the grapevine. It will amaze you to see how long people hold onto organizational brochures or your phone number. When they are ready, they will seek you out. Or they will pass along the information to other people. Time is on your side.

Technique Options

We are about to look at a wide variety of recruiting techniques in some depth. This is your "menu" of options from which to select the best way to tap a possible source of volunteers. So that you know up front, here is an outline of the techniques we are about to discuss:

Mass media
—Television and radio
—Newspapers
—Billboards

Special circulation publications

Public speaking
—Organized and random groups
—Speakers bureau

Slide shows and videotapes

Booths and exhibits
—Volunteer fairs

Direct mail

Referrals

Registering everywhere

Special events
—Piggybacking
—Creating events

Unclassifiable

THE VOLUNTEER RECRUITMENT BOOK/ELLIS

Pre-application orientation programs

One-to-one

Modern technology
—800 numbers
—Computer bulletin boards
—Fax

And then, in Chapter 8, we will cover (with illustrations):

Printed materials
—Brochures
—Flyers
—Posters
—Inserts and special items

As you will see, there are endless variations within all these broad categories. For each technique, I will try to present pluses and minuses to consider, and to offer some practical suggestions for making it work for you.

Weighing the Costs

You will have to determine whether the costs balance the returns for any of the techniques in this chapter. Costs include more than the cash expense of producing a recruitment tool or doing a mailing. How much time will this technique require to plan, produce, and deliver? Your time? Other employee or volunteer time? What is the energy expenditure needed?

Another variable is how many volunteers you require. If you have an opening for one volunteer, you clearly want to select a technique that does not demand a great deal of effort (yet that is successful). But if you need fifteen volunteers, you can justify more time and expense.

One recommendation is never to do a recruitment task if it only serves one purpose. As a busy person, you can rarely afford to put a lot of effort into a one-shot technique. But if you can adapt the same speech for several audiences, or can use the same slides for both recruitment and new volunteer orientation, then you can justify your time.

In the same vein, try not to approach volunteer recruitment presentations too narrowly. Because of the "sowing seeds" reality discussed above, you may have to wait awhile for an appli-

cant to emerge after a presentation. Therefore, consider volunteer recruitment as a form of *public education*. You are building the public image of your organization, informing people about the work you do, and laying the groundwork for future advocacy, fundraising, and—yes—volunteer recruitment. So your activities do have a long-term, significant purpose even if your monthly report does not tally a high number of new applicants right away.

Let's look at each technique in depth.

The Mass Media

The "mass media" includes television, radio, newspapers, and billboards—but each category has important subdivisions. You know this already, but it helps to be as clear as possible when considering whether any part of the mass media will work for you as a recruitment technique.

Television and radio each have commercial broadcasting stations, either network-affiliated or local. There are also public broadcasting stations. Television is now increasingly affected by cable and satellite dish, through which stations from very far away can be brought into a local area.

Depending on the size of your community, there may be one or several major newspapers, both daily and weekly. You may also have a number of community or neighborhood newspapers, as well as a wide array of special audience papers such as those in foreign languages. Newspapers may be circulated on a newsstand, by subscription, or even distributed free of charge.

Television, radio and newspapers offer the recruiter a number of options:

Feature stories: These are stories written/produced to inform or entertain the reader/viewer. Usually a feature story is written by a reporter though some small stations or papers may consider using something you have developed yourself, if it is well-written or produced. Cable television might air a program you create entirely in-house, as part of its public access mandate (see below). Feature stories should be current but usually are the type that could be aired or printed at any time.

News stories: Similar to feature stories but must be "today's" event, i.e., *the news.*

Interviews: Usually broadcast, there are many talk shows seeking someone to interview who has something interesting to share with an audience. The national shows like Donahue or Oprah are very competitive (and probably won't find you many local volunteers!), but locally-originating talk shows frequently seek new guests and have a surprisingly wide audience, even at the oddest hours of airing.

In general, mass media is an avenue for *publicity* and can be used to make people aware of any aspect of your organization and its work. Also, the public must become familiar with your organization before you can ask people to give their time to it. But to make mass media work as a *recruitment* tool, you have to be explicit about your message: inviting people to volunteer. Publicity and recruitment are connected, but they are not the same thing.

Pros and Cons

There are pluses and minuses in using the mass media as a recruitment technique. On the plus side:

1. The mass media allow you to get your message to many people at once, at low cost to you. But you must be prepared to do the necessary screening that results from many inquiries.

2. If you select the right show or paper for your needs, the mass media is a way to speak directly to the type of prospective volunteer you want to find. An appearance on daytime television will be seen by people available in the daytime. A message delivered during a Spanish talk show will be understood by people who speak Spanish. These are ways to "target" your audience using the mass media.

3. Mass media is great for what I call the "needle in the haystack" search. Some skills are so rare that you just can't brainstorm "where we can find people with this skill." So going "public" gives you a fighting chance to cast your net and find the one or two people with that ability. A true life example occurred in central Pennsylvania more than twenty years ago. Camp Indiantown Gap was selected by the U.S. Government as a holding area for Vietnam and Cambodian refugees. The social service agen-

cies in that very rural area needed to locate—quickly and for a three-month period—volunteers able to speak Indochinese languages. The mass media spread the word effectively and brought out surprising resources.

But the mass media also requires caution! While it can provide you with nice publicity, it is what I call "indiscriminate" recruiting—you must screen candidates carefully because they will not be coming from a known source. Because of this, for most situations, the mass media is not the technique of first choice. It certainly is not the technique you want to use if you only need one or two volunteers to fill certain slots (except for the "needle in the haystack" situation already mentioned).

Another concern is that you can rarely control what the media says about you. So any story presented by a reporter or interviewer has the risk of sending the wrong message or one with inaccurate information. The timing and placement of a story may also be factors that work against reaching the audience you most want to address. (So if you want to reach people who can help you in the evening after work, it may not be helpful to go on a morning talk show when those people are at work and can't be listening.)

The natural impulse is to make the most of mass media exposure and advertise too many options. Listeners and readers cannot absorb a complicated message while skimming or channel surfing. If you do use the mass media, discipline yourself to *focus* on *one* volunteer opportunity at a time. It is also important to stress the *volunteer assignment available*, not the description of your agency.

In rural areas, your media choices are more limited—but then everyone reads or listens to the same materials. In larger and urban communities, the largest media outlets may actually be the worst options for volunteer recruitment. It is easy for your message to get lost. Instead, do some research on what might be a myriad of neighborhood and special interest publications. These smaller venues often welcome new material and like to help volunteer causes. If you have volunteers or members from the neighborhood the publication covers, build a story around them. This doubles up some nice volunteer recognition with a legitimate "see what our neighbors are doing'' story.

There are a number of excellent books available to teach you how to write good press releases or to design interesting news stories. Recruit a journalism student or a public relations consultant to work with you in contacting the mass media. Develop relationships with reporters, editors, and general managers, especially in a smaller community. They might be willing to work with you to develop your ''newsworthiness.''

The general wisdom is that photographs accompanying a story make it more appealing. Also, editors like to know if a story produced any results—if you received a number of inquiries about volunteer openings after a story came out, let the paper or station know. And always send a thank you note for any publicity provided!

Creating News

Sometimes you can create a news story without actually doing anything new! The key is to piggyback onto a news story gaining attention somewhere else. If you can show your local media that you are involved in something that has captured the audience's attention, you will get coverage. For example, if a missing child case is on the front page, point out that your organization is working every day to protect the neighborhood or to give latchkey children a safe place to go after school.

If this sounds like ambulance chasing, realize that the same approach works for ''good news'' stories, too. Is someone famous turning ninety today? Why not send a press release pointing out the two volunteers who also turned ninety this year.

A similar technique is to connect with a national event. Arbor Day may sound old-fashioned, but if your group plants trees you can give the local media a photo opportunity for this ''holiday.'' When the national media covers the White House Easter Egg Hunt, why not suggest your local television station or newspaper cover the visit of the Easter Bunny to your nursing home? Do your best to make sure mention of the ways volunteers are needed is added in to the general publicity attention.

To return to the current events theme, a local tie-in with a natural disaster half way across the country (flood, earthquake, or any other attention-

grabber) might be to discuss how the emergency rescue squad *here* is preparing for the worst . . . and is looking for a few good volunteers.

Finally, you can make news with some sort of celebrity endorsement. Whether a sports figure, movie star, or politician, some names will automatically get media attention. But fame is fleeting and you must be careful to weigh all considerations: the reputation of this celebrity in his or her private and public life, other causes to which s/he may be connected, if the endorsement is given as a volunteer or for money, and whether the endorsement is one-time or ongoing (and whether you want it to be either).

Advertising in the Mass Media

There are several ways to use the mass media to advertise your message. An ad gives you more control over content than an article or broadcast news story but, because of the short word count or brief air time, advertising forces you to say your message succinctly. Here are your choices:

Public service advertising: There was a time when all commercial radio and television stations were required by law to air public service advertising, usually known as ''spots'' or ''PSAs.'' No more. The good news, however, is that most stations see such ads as a valid community service and want to air them—but not as frequently as before and not at times that paid advertising fills the schedule.

Cable television, on the other hand, receives its license by local government contract and, in most areas, the politicians have insisted on what is called ''public access'' time. Community bulletin boards (yes, those that air the high school lunch menu for the week) abound, as do locally-produced shows. The key is that most cable companies are required to loan out video equipment, teach you how to use it, and air your productions—providing you represent a bona fide non-profit organization! So you might consider recruiting some volunteers with video production skills to create a half-hour show for you that will have several purposes: to be aired on the cable station, but also to be used as part of your public speaking repertoire (see below), to orient new volunteers, and as volunteer recognition. Even though cable public access channels have low viewership, you can be certain that you are speaking to local people.

Paid advertising: If you buy publication space or airtime, you have complete control over the content and placement of your ad. Some volunteer programs have had good success using the *classified* section of the newspaper. This is useful if you are looking for someone to fill an intensive volunteer assignment. Do not advertise under "V" for "Volunteer." Place the ad under its relevant job title: Project Coordinator, Library Organizer, Computer Consultant. In the text of the ad, note clearly that this is a volunteer or unpaid position.

Shared ad space: One way that a local business can help your cause would be to donate part of its ad space to your appeal for volunteers. For example, a pharmacy with a lot of senior customers might be willing to say: "Smith's Drugs applauds Meals on Wheels and reminds you that many of our customers depend on their neighbors for a daily hot meal. Might you be willing to volunteer? Call 555-4321 for more details." The rest of the ad would be devoted to the ordinary selling of products and services. Like celebrity endorsements, you need to pick your business partners carefully. But this is one way to reach a wide audience at no cost to you.

Regular volunteer recruitment "columns": Sometimes coordinated by a Volunteer Center but sometimes run by the newspaper itself, many communities have a weekly or monthly regular feature that is a great help to volunteer recruiters. Generally five to ten organizations are permitted to submit a short description of a volunteer opportunity. So this is like a specialized want-ad column. Readers tend to become familiar with the feature and glance it over regularly. If you have the chance to participate in such a column, remember the guideline about focusing. Select *one* volunteer job description and highlight that one well.

Special media campaigns: Usually organized by a national organization or by an umbrella group such as the United Way, periodically there are mass media campaigns designed to *raise awareness* about volunteering among the general public. Re-

cent examples are the Independent Sector's "Give Five" campaign or the Points of Light Foundation's 800-number spots. As one agency, you will probably have little input about what is said or when it is aired. But you might be able to get access to the campaign's logo or literature and produce your own material piggybacking upon the campaign. Or see if the local station will do a feature on your agency as a way to "personalize" the national message.

Billboards range from the massive signs along the side of a highway to small placards in buses and trains. They can be commercially rented or privately posted. Remember the "Uncle Sam Wants *You*" wartime figure? Billboards *can* communicate! This is generally an expensive recruitment technique, unless someone donates *both* the space and the sign(s) themselves. Also, you will need a professional designer to help you get your message across in one picture and only a few words. But for some situations, such ads can be effective.

Special Circulation Publications

While the mass media is fraught with frustrations, a much more fruitful avenue to consider is special circulation publications. These are newsletters and other regularly-produced items that are published for specific audiences. So if you choose the right forum for your message, the people who read it will all be possible volunteer candidates. Special circulation publications include:

- In-house newsletters (house organs) published as internal documents for corporations and large nonprofits reaching all employees or sometimes even targeted to specific departments or groups within the company.
- Foreign language newspapers.
- Association newsletters and bulletins reaching all the members of a group.
- School newspapers.
- Professional newsletters and journals.

Just as with the mass media, you can seek feature stories or ads from such special publications. Usually you start by contacting the editor and discussing why you think your message is of particular interest to his/her readers. If the editor agrees, you can work together to decide the best way to spread the word. Some newsletters already have a "community bulletin board" column or classified section that can be adapted to your recruitment information.

It is helpful to develop short articles and even succinct paragraphs that could be printed as is by a busy editor. Well-worded press releases get attention, too. Also, develop some eye-catching "camera-ready" ads of different column widths that could be inserted into any newsletter.

Public Speaking

Volunteer recruiters can easily fill their schedules with speaking engagements. In every community there are all sorts of organizations seeking luncheon and dinner speakers—eager Program Committee Chairs are always searching for interesting topics to offer at a monthly meeting. Your challenge is to accept or elicit only the most fruitful speaking engagements that have potential to lead you to the volunteers you want to recruit.

Do your homework! Be sure you know who will be in your audience and why you are there. Remember, you won't find black men at a Swedish women's club! So be sure to ask your contact person:

- Who will be in the audience? What are their ages, sex, race, religion, background, etc.?
- How many people are expected?
- What other speakers have they heard recently?
- Do members of this group have a history of volunteering, either as individuals or as part of an organization-sponsored group community service project?

Also ask logistical questions to help you prepare your presentation:

- Exactly how much time will you have? Where will you fit on the agenda? What will happen before and after you speak?
- What will the room be like? Should you expect a dark, formal auditorium? a bright, noisy lunchroom?

- Where will you speak? Will you have a podium? be on a stage?
- Will you have access to a microphone? To an overhead projector or slide projector (or any other audiovisual equipment you may need to bring if it is not available on site)?
- Will there be a table on which you can display anything? Can someone help to distribute handout materials?
- Is there some place you can stay behind and meet with interested people after the meeting?

Most groups are happy to accommodate your needs as a speaker—if you specify them in advance. Never assume that you know the details of a speaking engagement. The time it takes to discuss the questions listed above will be very well spent.

If you are uncomfortable or unfamiliar with public speaking, work in tandem with a volunteer or other colleague who can help you out. Read some of the books on the subject . . . or take a workshop or community college course. This is a life skill that is worthwhile to learn, whatever your career goals.

Where to Speak

Select your speaking engagements with care. There are two types of groups to which you can speak: organized groups and random or "unaffiliated" groups.

Organized groups include churches and other religious congregations, civic clubs such as Rotary or Soroptimists, professional societies such as associations of CPAs or Public Relations Directors, and special interest clubs such as horticulture societies. All of these groups share the following characteristics:

- They are made up of *members*—people who joined the group to be with peers and friends and for whom the meetings, and therefore the speakers, are simply an interesting aspect of group involvement. These organization or club members may not be looking for additional volunteering to do. Be careful that you are not just this week's nice luncheon speaker.

- They have their own recruitment needs to find new members and to encourage current members to become more active. Your recruitment needs may, in fact, conflict with theirs.

- They may be approached numerous times throughout the year by recruiters such as yourself and therefore have developed creative ways of saying "no" to requests for help.

- They will respond to project ideas that serve *their* needs while also serving the needs of others. So if you want to get an organized group to help you, figure out how to engage them *as* a group (even though individual members are always free to become interested in volunteering for you as well).

Random groups can be found at a variety of sites. You are looking for places where a group of people are gathered, have time to listen, share some common interest that brought them together, but are "unaffiliated" with each other beyond that particular event. Examples of random groups are participants in a workshop or conference, students in a classroom, visitors at an open house, or people attending a lecture, film, or sporting event. For volunteer recruitment purposes, the "unaffiliated" group may hold more potential than the organized group because the characteristics are flipped around:

- Listeners are not necessarily already committed to something as a member or volunteer and therefore might be open to hearing about their opportunities to become involved.

- If you have targeted the right event, you are speaking to people who share an interest in the topic under consideration that day. So if you speak at an animal rights conference about volunteering with the Humane Society, there is a logic to your approach.

Designing Your Presentation

One very important tip: do *not* bill yourself as a speaker about volunteer opportunities! It sounds boring (and probably is) to come hear someone talk about volunteering. Also, advertising

that you plan to recruit volunteers is likely to have a reverse-psychology effect! You are warning people to sit on their hands and be very careful not to get "sucked in"! Remember that most people feel over-extended and tend to subscribe to the old military stereotype of "never volunteer."

So what do you speak about? It's simple. You will speak about your organization and its work, with the goal of being an informative and even provocative presenter. Think about the trends and issues your organization addresses or is affected by. Build your presentation around those, with special attention to things that might be a surprise to your audience. Then, *within the context* of your remarks, mention the things volunteers are doing.

When I spoke on behalf of the Family Court volunteer program, I included topics such as:

—Statistics on juvenile crime in Pennsylvania and in Philadelphia; an overview of the types of youngsters seen by the Court and the delinquency and dependency issues that might bring them there.

—How probation services work and what the challenges are.

—The greatest needs of the clients the volunteer program sees.

—How the Philadelphia media affects juvenile crime.

—What the average citizen can do to help the problem of families in trouble.

In other words, I was a speaker about juvenile crime in Philadelphia. I was engaged in community education first and volunteer recruitment second. If someone in my audience was not interested in the information I had to share, then that person was an unlikely candidate to be a prospective volunteer. Conversely, someone who found my presentation of great interest would be more likely to be intrigued by the opportunity (often unexpected) to become personally involved.

So a speaking engagement allows audience members to *self-screen* their interest. Recruitment occurs as a natural extension of people's attraction to the subject—and that means that not everyone (in fact only a minority) will respond as prospective volunteers.

I want to clarify that you are welcome to *end*

your presentation with a "recruitment pitch." You might say: "During my talk I mentioned a number of ways volunteers are helping our organization to do its work. Let me take a moment to tell you about some of the needs we currently have for more volunteers. I'll be happy to discuss these with you individually afterwards."

Unscientifically, my anecdotal research over the years has led me to believe that a speaking engagement is successful as a volunteer recruitment technique if you get *one* volunteer from the effort! So view the activity from a broader perspective or you will quickly get very frustrated.

An Exception to the Rule

One of the reviewers of the manuscript of this book, Maggi Davern, made a margin note in response to the preceding recommendation not to concentrate your speeches on the subject of volunteering. She noted that she is increasingly being *invited* to speak about volunteer opportunities at her agency (Catholic Social Services in Minneapolis), particularly when the audience is students. And, of course, she is right. In Chapter 5 we discussed the growing trend of school-based community service. As people (of any age) become aware of the potential of volunteer service, you may well be asked to do overt recruiting at a school, senior group, or any other setting. Go for it! However, the point I made above is still relevant to many speeches, especially if you are the one seeking out the chance at the podium.

If you are planning to deliver a speech about volunteerism—especially if you are representing a Volunteer Center or other organization trying to influence the public's concept of who volunteers are and what they do—surprise your listeners with facts and stories not often shared. Use reports such as the Gallup Poll data about statistical trends in volunteering.[1] Recount historical anecdotes about the achievements of volunteers, many of which are not identified as such. (Who created the Boston Tea Party? Who ran the Underground Railroad? Who funded the renovation of the Statue of Liberty? Volunteers!) Katie Noyes and I wrote *By the People: A History of Americans as Volunteers* (Jossey-Bass, 1990) for exactly this use by public speakers.

More Public Speaking Tips

In general, sincerity wins out over technique every time. Audiences have an uncanny ability to hear genuine enthusiasm, warmth and commitment, even from a nervous speaker. But there are ways to help yourself along. You can increase the impact of your presentation with slides (see below) or by bringing along a current volunteer who can give personal testimony as to the value of being a volunteer with your organization.

Come prepared to discuss options for involvement with any organized group. This is sometimes more effective than asking a group if they are willing to accept a specific assignment. The answer to that question has a 50% chance of being "no." Instead, if appropriate, engage the full group in the question: "What are some ways your organization might help our clients/organization?" By asking an open-ended question like this, you are collaborating with the group. They may think of ways to help that you have not considered. At a minimum, they might write you a check.

Always have handouts to leave with people after your speech that contain your name and telephone number. People hang on to these things for an amazing period of time, or they pass them along to others, and so you will be sowing those seeds for the future by putting such paper into circulation. When time and money permit, make handouts specific to that particular audience. Start with something like: "To participants in the October 3 Workshop." Computers help a lot these days—keep basic handouts in a data file and alter them with a few keystrokes.

Stick around after your speech to talk to audience members individually. Speak to the group's officers and keep discussing what they might like to do *as a group* to help out.

Speakers Bureaus

If you feel that live presentations are an effective technique for your recruitment effort and if there are many groups to whom you hope to speak, you will either have to clone yourself or form a "speakers bureau"! Whether you give it such a fancy name or not, the concept of a speakers bureau is to develop a pool of people who are skilled in public speaking and trained to make consistent presentations on your behalf.

Current volunteers who are good at sharing their personal experiences can be effective recruiters. But you can also utilize people whose major volunteer job is being on your speakers bureau. Handling one or two speaking engagements for you may be a great way to keep people involved even if other commitments require them to reduce other volunteer activities with you. Current and past board members and other agency employees are candidates for the bureau, too.

It is imperative that you train speakers bureau participants. Never assume you know what someone will say or that each person will say the same thing every time. Work together to create a consistent outline (try to avoid a fully-written speech). Talk to each other before each presentation to discuss how to adapt the speech to that particular audience.

Volunteer speakers can go out alone or in pairs. But if two people go together, be sure they decide in advance who will do which part of the presentation.

Slide Shows/Videotapes

A picture is worth a thousand words. Pictures reflect your image: people of all races and both sexes enjoying their work, productive activity, etc. Visual materials also tell your story, demonstrate what goes on in your organization, and answer questions. Do people wonder what your facility looks like? Show them.

One clever director of volunteers at an urban hospital diagnosed correctly that prospective volunteers were concerned about their personal safety outside of the hospital after dark. She obtained permission from neighboring buildings to go up to their roofs and photograph the hospital from all around. Then, in a matter of fact way, she incorporated slides of the hospital's adjacent, well-lit parking lot into her recruitment presentation. People commented to her that they were relieved to learn they could walk to and from their cars with security.

Slides are quite inexpensive to produce and have great flexibility. You can mix and match them for whatever audience you are addressing, and you can keep adding updated shots. You can change the narration as you go along, or you can script the presentation so that anyone can deliver it consistently. Or, someone with a wonderful speaking voice can tape record the narration for a more professional sound.

If you have the right equipment, a slide/tape show can be "orchestrated" with automatic slide cues and even multi-projector effects. Also, you can purchase a self-contained system that runs continuously by itself and can be used on a table-top display.

Carry a camera with you as often as possible and capture volunteer activities as they occur. Slides have the most uses, but photographs can end up on displays and on printed materials. Recruit one or more volunteers to be official program photographers. Recruit a professional photographer to create a "starter set" of slides as a special project for you. Of course you will be happy to add a closing slide listing the names of everyone who contributed their efforts. Offer to pay for the film and the developing—the real donation here is time and skill.

Videotapes are far more complicated and expensive. Also, people have increasingly high expectations these days about video quality. If you have the chance to have a video made for you, by all means say yes, but you may not need to be this sophisticated with your audiovisual tools. As already noted, cable television stations can be a great resource for producing your own videos at little cost. But it takes much more skill to shoot and edit a good videotape than to create nice slides.

The real drawback of a videotape is its lack of flexibility. The scenes must be shown in the same sequence every time, taking the same number of minutes each time. If something changes or is outdated, you're stuck with it.

On the other hand, a "home" video can be quite effective if it is presented in context. So show a brief tape of last month's tutor/student party just to capture its flavor. Then move on to more polished material.

See if you can recruit a community group or business to underwrite the cost of creating your slide show or video, or try to recruit an advertising firm or student class to actually produce one for you. Larger corporations have media departments that might help, as do larger nonprofit organizations. Is there something you might barter with your local hospital or university in exchange for access to their editing equipment?

Keep in mind that audiovisual materials you create for volunteer recruitment purposes have other valuable uses. You can show them during new volunteer orientation or training events. And they are marvelous at volunteer recognition events, especially if you keep adding new slides that serve as sort of a "year in review." People love to see themselves in pictures. Aim to show as many volunteers in the shots as possible each year, use all the slides at the recognition event, and then edit the set down for recruitment purposes.

Booths and Exhibits

Every community has opportunities for setting up some sort of exhibit in a public place. You might be exhibiting alone or with many other booths. In order to make use of this recruitment option, you must create an exhibit that represents you well. Although you can spend a great deal of money on display boards, it is possible to design a low-cost exhibit that does the job for you. As with the other techniques we have been discussing, start by looking for a volunteer with some experience in creating exhibit booths and you will not have to struggle alone.

Most of the time you will be using table-top exhibits. Here are some things to consider:

- Will you be staffing the exhibit all the time or will the materials be unattended? If unattended, do you want a passive exhibit or something more interactive such as a self-running slide show?

- How can you make the materials portable, lightweight and durable? (You will want to use the basic exhibit materials as often as possible.)

- Will the public be walking all around the exhibit or just in front?

- How can you get some height in the materials so that the display will be visible from a distance?

- How can you create banners or posters that are adaptable to different ways of being mounted?

- Which parts of the exhibit will be considered permanent versus those parts that can be changed to suit each venue?

Obviously budget, time available, and artistic talent will affect all of your choices.

Once you have determined your physical format, your biggest challenge (as always) is to *focus your message*. Is this exhibit trying to accomplish more than one thing? For example, it is common to use a booth to explain an organization's services to prospective *clients* as well as to do volunteer recruitment. So you need to design the exhibit to communicate as clearly as possible. For example, perhaps you can divide the space so that your volunteer recruitment message is separated from the other information.

It is vital to have printed materials that visitors to your table can take away with them. Rarely will people take the time to read everything on the spot. You can also give people the option of signing up for more information to be sent later. This gives you the benefit of obtaining their names and addresses for more personal outreach and follow-up.

The benefits of an exhibit depend on where you place it. If you participate in community-wide events such as shopping mall fairs, you can hope for increased visibility but have to accept the fact that the majority of people will care little about your work. If you have found a spot within an event targeted to your interests (such as the car rally we discussed earlier), you will be meeting a large number of people with great potential to fill your needs. Because staffing a booth takes enormous time, this recruitment option may be too costly (in the time and energy to staff it) when weighed against the likely payback.

So your most important decision is selecting the right place to put your exhibit. As discussed in the chapter on where to look for volunteers, you can ask to include a volunteer recruitment table at an already-scheduled community event, "piggybacking" on the work of others to get out a crowd. The variety of such events is endless, from Job Opportunity Expositions for high school seniors to Home Shows for do-it-yourselfers. Work with your potential source of volunteers to determine the best type of exhibit, timing, etc. for that location.

Then adapt your exhibit as much as possible to each location, such as changing photographs to show scenes of greatest interest to that audience.

Volunteer Fairs

Exhibiting can be directly focused on volunteer recruitment if you participate in a "Volunteer Fair" with other agencies. Such an event is often sponsored by a local Volunteer Center or by a host company or college. The idea is to generate interest in community service by a neighborhood, group of employees, or student body. Although you will be one booth among many, all of whom are trying to recruit volunteers, the "competition" is actually less than it seems. Visitors to the fair will usually self-screen the booths they visit based on their personal interests. So if you have volunteer opportunities for working with children, people who really prefer helping seniors will bypass you while those wanting to work with children will stop and visit.

Direct Mail

There are three types of direct mail volunteer recruiting. You can send a mass mailing to a targeted mailing list, you can enclose a special letter or flyer in a mailing being produced by someone else, and you can send personalized letters to selected individuals.

Mass mailings can be expensive and only make sense as a recruitment option if you have faith in the quality of the mailing list. For example, if you want to recruit volunteers to prepare income tax returns for senior citizens and you can obtain the addresses of all retired CPAs in your county, a mailing might produce results. It may not make any difference if the letters are sent first class or third class, so stretch your budget accordingly.

More useful and less expensive for you is an enclosure in a mailing already being sent for other reasons. Here you avoid the postage costs and get the benefit of an implied endorsement from the initiating organization. As always, you will get the best results if you know exactly whom you want to reach and focus your letter or flyer to that audience. So when all the members of the literary society open their quarterly mailing, they will find a letter from you explaining how they can translate their love of books into helping others to learn how to read.

Personalized letters, always sent first class, are usually used as step one of a two-step approach. You send only as many letters each week as you can follow up with a personal phone call the next week. Personal letters introduce your organization to the recipient. You can either be trying to recruit that person directly or you may want that person to be a conduit for you to a larger group of prospective volunteers. This leads us to the technique of "referrals."

Referrals

Key community leaders can be invaluable allies in your recruitment efforts. These are people in a position to identify likely prospective volunteers for you to contact. In some cases, your referral sources may even make the initial contact for you. So your challenge is to enlist the support of the person in the leadership position—you must show her or him how helping you will also help the group for which the leader is responsible.

Here are some examples:

- *Clergy* can find appropriate congregation members to volunteer for you if they see the link between such service and a chance to foster lay ministry or do new member outreach.

- *Association officers* may organize groups of their members to help you if the projects also meet the goals of their organization or give them visibility in the community.

- *Public affairs personnel* of corporations will identify skilled employees for your needs if such involvement will give the company a good reputation or make employees feel recognized.

- *College professors* will encourage their students to volunteer for you if they see how students will gain a practical understanding of classroom theory.

Meet your referral sources half way by giving them tools to use in recruiting for you. Along with your cover letter or during your meeting, give the person a set of flyers to distribute or post on bulletin boards.

A variation on the idea of referrals that requires less commitment on the part of your community contact is simply gaining *access* to potential recruits through that contact. Can the person arrange for you to speak briefly at a meeting? Is there a bulletin board on which you can post a flyer? Is there a place to leave brochures where people might have the time to read them (waiting rooms in doctors' offices, vestibules of churches, etc.)? In essence, such contact people are endorsing your organization by permitting this access, so their help is tangible.

Registering Everywhere

In Chapter 6 on "Where to Look for Volunteers," we discussed listing your volunteer opportunities with every possible clearinghouse and directory, making maximum use of referral systems already in place. Such volunteer referral services are potential sources of volunteers—keeping yourself listed with them all is a technique of recruitment.

Special Events

We have already praised the virtues of piggybacking onto a special event occurring in your community. Another technique is to *create* an event designed to gain visibility for volunteer opportunities in your organization. These can range from car washes to balloon launches. The idea is to generate enthusiasm and attention, while finding ways to distribute literature or explain the volunteer assignment openings. Select an event with some logical connection to your volunteer needs: car washes for finding drivers, craft shows for resident knitting circle leaders, etc. Is your event likely to attract young people? Families? Is this the audience you want to reach?

A more focused variation of this idea is holding an open house, sponsoring a lecture or workshop, or convening a public forum—all designed to educate the public about issues important to your organization. The event becomes an end unto itself, in that everyone attending should gain knowledge and understanding. As a volunteer recruitment technique, this type of event draws out people who self-identify their interest in the subject—which makes them a candidate to become a volunteer. Place an exhibit about volunteer opportunities in the lobby, distribute special flyers, and use the podium to make a *brief* presentation at the end of the program. Or, be sure there is an attendance list with names and addresses and send a personal note to everyone afterwards, welcoming them to inquire about volunteering opportunities.

The time and effort required to plan and carry off special events can be enormous, so be sure you know what message you want to convey. Set goals for the type of people you want to reach, in what numbers, and with what follow-up.

Unclassifiable

Because I cannot predict the results of your brainstorming session on the best places to look for volunteers, I also cannot guess the many unique ways you may invent to get your recruiting message to the prospects at a particular source. You and your contact person at that site will have to be creative.

For example, if you have decided that a local supermarket has potential as a recruitment site for the type of volunteer you need, there are any one of a number of ways to attract the attention of shoppers. You could use some of the techniques we've already discussed, such as: have cashiers stuff a message into grocery bags, post a flyer on the market's community bulletin board, or ask the market to print your recruitment message in its weekly "specials" newspaper insert. But you might also consider:

- Having volunteers in tee-shirts with your organization's logo pack groceries, take the bags to people's cars, and then hand out a flyer.
- Staff a table just outside or inside the door with free hot coffee and tea (winter) or cold drinks (summer), with a banner saying something like: "We wanted to do something nice for you . . . can you do something nice for us?"

A number of years ago, in an attempt to recruit volunteer drivers, a social service agency in a small town engaged the help of the two gas stations on Main Street. First, the agency hung a banner across the road announcing their campaign to find drivers (of course they got permission from the township to do this). Then, on one Saturday, they placed teenaged volunteers in logo tee-shirts at both gas stations to wipe car windows (front, back, and sides). Because this was a small community, many of the drivers recognized some of the teens. Conversations happened naturally. And everyone drove off with a flyer describing the volunteer position of driver.

The day required a lot of work to plan and execute. Some volunteers were indeed recruited, but the agency also gained a great deal of positive publicity. The kids kept the tee-shirts as a thank you and the unexpected result was that they kept wearing them! So the public relations effort extended over more months than had been planned.

What "unclassifiable" technique might you dream up to match the potential of a source of prospective volunteers? A Volunteer Center might plan a parade for next year's recognition event—floats would describe the things volunteers do in the community and the marchers would be volunteers themselves. This would certainly show the sheer numbers of citizens involved! Now, if every one of the marchers was given ten recruitment flyers to distribute to spectators en route . . . !

Pre-application Orientation Programs

Some volunteer programs have had success in recruiting volunteers by scheduling regular "orientation" programs to which anyone expressing an interest in volunteer opportunities is invited. While normally an orientation occurs after a screening interview and just before actual placement, the technique of offering the session before an application is filed is useful if prospects may have misconceptions about the agency or its clients, or many questions about the work. The orientation session then becomes a way for people to self-screen prior to requesting an application form.

If you use this technique, you can use general press releases or more targeted materials to "announce" orientation dates and times—and then see who shows up. But it is important to clarify that attending the session creates neither an obligation to apply for a volunteer position nor a guarantee of acceptance as a volunteer.

One-to-One

As we have already discussed under "referrals," sometimes a well-worded letter or phone call to a key contact person will result in just the right referral. This idea leads us to what some believe to be the most significant recruitment technique of all: one-to-one recruiting by satisfied volunteers of their friends and contacts. There is no substitute for personal conviction. A person with direct experience as a volunteer can communicate enthusiasm in a believable way.

If you want current volunteers to recruit more volunteers, *ask them to do so!* Don't just passively hope for their help. Create opportunities for volunteers to introduce their circle of contacts to you and give them the tools to spread your message. For example, invite current volunteers to bring their friends or relatives to a special event (an open house or a presentation by a guest lecturer) to learn more about your organization. No obligation implied! This is important. Volunteers may be willing to introduce their friends to you, but may not want to "make the pitch." Conversely, you must clarify that you will screen all applicants. Just because a volunteer recommends a friend should not mean automatic acceptance into the position.

Consider combining a recognition event with a recruitment opportunity. Hold an ice cream sundae party for volunteers to which they may bring up to three friends, if they wish. Use the time to give genuine thanks to the volunteers (it may be even nicer for them to shine in front of their friends), and add a few words to "our guests" about volunteering at your organization. Then give all guests an informational flyer.

Volunteers are not your only one-to-one asset. As appropriate, ask current *clients* to talk to their family and friends about the work of your organization—and give them flyers to take home that describe your search for volunteers. As we discussed already in Chapter 6, your "sphere of influence" is greater than it seems and you may be missing opportunities to give people the chance to help.

Do special outreach to *alumni,* either past volunteers or past participants/clients. Perhaps you can invite them to do something *specific* for you, such as participate in a one-time volunteer activity, rather than asking in a vague way for "support." Separate volunteer recruitment from fundraising.

Finally, be aware of the main danger of relying on one-to-one recruitment: it tends to keep the volunteer corps homogeneous. People are related to people who look like themselves, have similar world views and backgrounds, and come from similar neighborhoods. And the same is likely true of their friends and work colleagues. So if you want to *diversify* your volunteer corps, you must first do active outreach to new ages, races, or whatever group is not yet represented. Once you have recruited enough representatives from different populations, you can then use the one-to-one approach to keep expanding your numbers. (For more on diversity, see Chapter 11.)

Telephone Technology

As time goes on, new techniques of recruitment present themselves. This is why it is so important to focus on the rationale for recruitment and not look for standard answers on "how" to recruit. When I first started doing workshops on recruitment nineteen years ago, cable television did not exist. Now it is an emerging player in the mass media arena and a viable recruitment option.

Ten years ago, the capability to launch a national media campaign using a *toll-free 800 number* was pie-in-the-sky and expensive. Today this mass media/telephone technology is within reach, even for a statewide campaign. Whether by television, radio, or some other mass market distribution mechanism such as corporate-sponsored messages printed on products, viewers/listeners/consumers are urged to call a central telephone number to learn more about a volunteer opportunity in their local community.

People do indeed respond to 800-number campaigns, but that is not the hard part! The biggest challenge is having an efficient system in place to handle a national phone-in campaign — enough phone lines, knowledgeable and pleasant people to answer the calls and, most important, real work available for prospective volunteers to do (not to mention local level capability to deal with an increased but unpredictable number of calls). Nothing turns people off from volunteering more than making a call that leads nowhere. Unfortunately, too many 800-number campaigns concentrate on the grand total of inquiries and not on whether people actually get connected to real assignments. Another concern is that national media "spots" highlight the most interesting types of volunteer work, implying that all volunteers will cuddle abandoned babies or be assigned to a lively youngster. The prospective volunteer responds to this appeal and then discovers that the actual assignments available locally are quite different.

There are many variations on national recruitment campaigns that have not yet been tried (and possibly not yet imagined). There is certainly potential for this to become a viable form of recruitment. If you are with a local affiliate of a national organization, I predict increased attention to such centralized recruitment in the future.

Recruiting by *fax machine* is another new technological idea. You can even use computer faxing or purchase a fax with "broadcast" abilities, sending one message to tens or hundreds of fax numbers simultaneously. Fax recruiting can be annoying because it is unsolicited and uses the prospects' paper stock. But if you fax to targeted people who perhaps have already indicated some interest in your work, you will indeed get their attention. It is therefore a good way to mobilize members or donors to take some specific action for you.

In general, the use of a fax indicates urgency. So use it only for immediate needs, close to deadline, as a way to galvanize one-time volunteer actions: "Tomorrow morning is the deadline for delivering your canned goods for the Thanksgiving baskets" or "Join us at City Hall for the big protest on Wednesday!"

Cyberspace

Computer technology is itself so new that, in the first edition of this book—a not-so-long six years ago—I could only predict briefly that it was an evolving volunteer recruitment technique that deserved to be watched. The main reason for the second edition and now this third one is that cyberspace has developed so quickly and dramatically that it demanded enlarged attention. Please turn to the new Appendix following page 140 for a full discussion of this amazing new recruitment technique.

The key point is that cyberspace is here to stay. E-mail, commercial online services, the Internet, the World Wide Web, and other electronic networks are all attracting literally millions of subscribers. Once the domain of hackers and academics, average folks are gaining affordable access to this form of communication. And, just as businesses are exploring commercial uses of this new marketplace, organizations seeking volunteers (and donors) are discovering how to get their message electronically to the most targeted audience. We're all learning together.

The Unknown Future

All of this leads us to...? None of us can predict the best volunteer recruitment techniques of the future. But the most successful recruiters will stay alert to all the trends...and might even pioneer a few ideas!

Another trend that has emerged since the first edition of this book (remember, only two short years!) is the growing number of national and state conferences of all types that are building in a community service opportunity for their conferees. The idea is to give something back to the host community, build esprit de corps among participants (a different way of getting acquainted), and offer a "practice what we preach" opportunity. Some service projects are brief, intensive bursts of activity scheduled around workshops at the conference. Sample activities might be children's book repair or park clean up. Other conferences will set aside a full day to complete a larger project such as building a playground. Be one of the first agencies to reach out consciously to such conference planners. Get on the calendar mailing list of your local Tourist Bureau or Chamber of Commerce for advance notice of scheduled conferences. Then contact the organizers and proactively offer a service project that seems to match their focus of interest.

Clearly the future will bring other emerging trends that evoke new or adapted recruitment techniques. Always remember that there are no rules, just possibilities!

---

[1]The Independent Sector commissions periodic Gallup Poll surveys about giving and volunteering. Contact IS at 1828 L Street, NW, Washington, DC 20036.

Techniques of Recruitment (Part Two) *Printed Materials*

Printed materials are the basic tools of your recruitment campaign. In some cases these materials must stand alone and convey your message directly. Other times you will be using printed materials to support or follow up more personal contacts. But remember my earlier observation that the inexperienced recruiter prints 5,000 brochures and then asks, "where should I put these?" Be sure that you do not waste time and money on unfocused recruitment tools. Go to print only when you know exactly how you will be using that piece of paper when it rolls off the press.

First let's examine the range of printed materials available for you to use.

Brochures: "Brochures" are formal, general descriptions of your entire program, filling several panels or pages in a typeset and printed format on heavier paper stock. This makes a brochure rather costly, so you want to have one that you can live with for at least a year or two. Because a brochure is general and lengthy, it is *not* a recruitment tool in and of itself. It is not flexible or adaptable for different targeted audiences. But a good brochure supports your outreach efforts, verifies that you are running a credible program, and works as a "response piece" when someone asks for more information. It is also very useful during prospective volunteer interviews, when you want to give candidates a feel for the scope of your program.

Flyers: "Flyers" are informal, single sheets of paper, generally inexpensively off-set printed or even photocopied, that you can target at specific sources of volunteers and/or to highlight specific volunteer

assignments. Flyers are meant to be distributed and read individually. They should have some headline and be visually appealing. You can combine graphics with several paragraphs of text or even a response coupon. Flyers can be used on bulletin boards, as inserts in mailings, as give-aways at exhibit tables, and in hundreds of other ways. A flyer might be created for one occasion only to follow up a speech, or might have a longer lifespan.

Through the magic of computers, you can develop a series of templates for basic flyers. Some to consider are:

—Handouts for after a presentation. Each time you can "personalize" the flyer with a current date and a headline such as "To the members of XYZ fraternity." The rest of the flyer might not change.

—Materials used at a tabletop exhibit. Again, you may only need to change the date and headline.

—Flyers "pitched" to students or to employees of a particular work site or to any other special target group.

Posters: "Posters" are signs ranging in size from small to very large, designed to catch the eye of the passer by and convey a brief message. Therefore, posters have limited usefulness as a recruitment tool because you cannot put much information on them. They can be placed in such places as store windows or on bulletin boards. Because schools use posters as educational tools, these are especially effective in reaching younger, student audiences.

Inserts and Special Items: "Inserts" are a specialized form of flyer that you tailor—and shape—as needed, such as bookmarks for use in libraries or bookstores, envelope stuffers, attachments to a factory's paychecks, etc. There are lots of variations! Depending on where you plan to spread your message, you can also print specialty items such as placemats, coasters, or other readable materials.

As with so many of these techniques, you will have to work with your *source* to develop the actual printed tool. For example, if you want to recruit by using the drive-in window of the local bank branch, you will want to let the bank determine what type of literature will work best at the window. If the department store is willing to include your message with their next advertising or billing to customers, the store will know what size piece you should design.

Guidelines for Printed Materials

For all printed materials, use the following guidelines:

1. Remember that it does not have to cost a lot to look neat and appealing. Also, your goal is to look good, not expensive.

2. Find someone with graphics talent to lay out your text, select type style, and help you to present the nicest look. Even with the tremendous asset of today's computer desktop publishing programs, there is no substitute for art talent and graphics expertise. (A word of caution, however: be honest with any artist, whether paid or volunteer, about your right of final approval. Not everyone will be able to convey the right tone or look and you have to feel comfortable turning down a design, even if it has been donated.)

3. Illustrations reflect on your organization. If you are using photographs, examine them carefully for the messages they convey. Are the people diverse in terms of age, race, sex? Do they look like they are having fun? working hard? posing for the camera? If you use drawings, weigh the different impressions made by cartoon-like characters versus more formal figures.

4. Avoid the word "volunteer" in a headline. As we discussed in Chapters 3 and 4, stereotypes about volunteering will interfere with getting your message across if the word "volunteer" is the first thing people see. Instead, use phrases like "get involved," or "become a part of." Even better are headlines that "grab" the reader—arousing curiosity to keep reading. Mention the volunteer job *title*, as in "be a tutor" or "*drive* people happy."

5. Do not imply that all candidates will be accepted into the volunteer position. Instead, ask people to "apply" or "call to talk about it."

6. Be upbeat. Stress what the volunteer will get as well as give.

7. Vocabulary sends a message, too. If you use lots of long words or formal language, you demonstrate the expectation that volunteers need some literacy or education. If you oversimplify your message, you may seem as if you are talking down to volunteers. Jargon or use of abbreviations implies that volunteers should already know something about your cause.

8. Color choice counts, both in paper stock and ink. Pink, while a lovely color, perpetuates the stereotype of volunteering as feminine. Day-glo brights might indicate a young, teen-oriented program. Gray, burgundy, and navy blue are more formal, serious colors. Your printer can explain the impact that colors have.

9. If you are going to print photographs, black ink on white paper makes them crisp and clear. Try to avoid printing photos in colored ink. The extra cost of a second color ink for headlines and highlighting will make the piece more attractive. (If your target audience is seniors, remember that black and white has a funereal look.)

10. Legibility must take priority over creativity. Your goal is to communicate, so avoid overly-artistic type styles that are hard to read. Size of type also affects legibility, of course. If your target audience is seniors, you may have to use somewhat larger or bolder type—and keep strong contrast between the color of ink and the color of the paper (note that red ink on pink paper is almost impossible for some older people to read).

11. The size of the finished piece must meet your needs. Will it be mailed and so should fit a standard-sized envelope? Should it match or contrast with the size of other agency brochures? In the illustrations section to come, note how Reading Urban Ministry selected a size to fit the literature racks in church vestibules.

12. Most prospective volunteers would prefer to telephone you for more information, so be sure to include your number (with area code). But if you supply some sort of response coupon or card for those prospects who want to start with more privacy, it is most effective to keep the message and amount of information requested short. This is not an "application." It is an indicator of interest or a request for further contact. Leave space for name, address, and day/evening phone numbers. Make the card a self-mailer or show the agency address prominently. (Then be sure you have a system for responding back!)

A good rule of thumb is to spend as much time mulling over the above decisions as you will be spending money on your printed item. So for your program brochure—probably the most expensive tool you develop—you should take all the time necessary to find artistic help, refine your text, and select the nicest look. For a one-time only flyer as a handout to thirty students after your classroom lecture, having almost anything will do the job! Except that it is *never* acceptable to have typographical errors or to look sloppy . . . and therefore uncaring. All printed materials must be *welcoming* if they are to succeed as volunteer recruitment tools.

A Word on Bulletin Boards

You will undoubtedly be placing your flyers on bulletin boards in many places. Select your location with care. It may seem like common wisdom to put your flyer on the bulletin board in the highest traffic area. But that may mean that your message will get lost among the hundreds of other notices posted there as well—or even get covered up by another layer of flyers. This is especially true on college campuses.

Try to find a bulletin board that will indeed be passed by the right target audience of potential volunteer recruits, but that has less visual competition. The board on the third floor may be seen by only half the people than the one in the main lobby, but your flyer upstairs has a fighting chance of actually been read!

Whenever possible, get permission to *staple* your flyer to the bulletin board instead of using thumb tacks. That way no one can abscond with your tacks for their flyer!

One useful idea is to include some type of tear-off coupon with the flyer. This might be a "pocket" with response forms people can send to you (though most people will prefer to telephone). Or you can use the old college trick of "fringing" the bottom (see the illustrated flyer headed "I'm 17 . . .") with your organization's name and phone number, allowing people to tear off one segment. This way, ten people can walk away with something in their hands to remind them to call you—without defacing or removing the flyer itself.

Just remember to keep posting fresh flyers periodically. This is good advice for just about any bulletin board you may want to use. Some places routinely purge their boards of anything that has been up for a few weeks. Keeping flyers current gives you the chance to update information as it changes (new vacancies in volunteer positions, for example). Date the flyer and use the fact that it is "fresh news" to gain attention.

Illustrations

The illustrations that follow were designed for a wide variety of volunteer settings, assignments, and target audiences. There is, of course, no such thing as a "perfect" recruitment tool and one can quibble with the details of any piece shown here. However, I have selected each because it illustrates (usually successfully) one or more of the points I have been discussing here and in Chapter 7. So I'll draw your attention to the things I like the most about each.

All are reprinted with permission of their source, unless the source could no longer be identified or located. Thanks to everyone for sharing their materials.

I'm 17, on probation and I can't read...

This statement is true of too many of the teenagers seen at Family Court. Can you be a reading tutor and friend to a probationer? We will train you to be an effective teacher. You give: your time as a volunteer; a commitment of two hours a week for at least six months; your interest and energy on behalf of your assigned teenager. You get: the satisfaction of knowing you are doing important work; training and experience that can count on a resume; an inside understanding of the juvenile justice system. If you are interested in learning more about how to become a Reading Tutor with the Special Services Office of the Philadelphia Family Court, call: ▮▮▮▮▮▮▮▮▮▮

SPECIAL SERVICES 555-7878 (×18)

Photocopied on 8 1/2" x 11" white paper, with headline hand drawn in colored magic marker. Bottom is fringed.

This was a bulletin board flyer we used in my Family Court program and I can attest to the fact that it successfully brought in applicants to become reading tutors to teenagers on probation. Luckily, none of the volunteers ever asked, "if the kid can't read, how come s/he can write?"! It is included here as an example of a very low-cost flyer, combining an arresting headline (no pun intended) with explanatory information. Originally designed by a volunteer, these flyers were hand-lettered by volunteers and posted by them mainly on bulletin boards in branch libraries (so we could target neighborhoods in which we most hoped to find tutors).

Note the "fringing" at the bottom so that interested people can conveniently tear off one small piece of the flyer and take away the phone number.

Draw from your past
to preserve our future

VOLUNTEER

with the
Fairfax County
Park Authority
Conservation Division

Lead children's programs to

- Kindle a love of nature
- Share your knowledge
- Foster a sense of stewardship
- Spark young imaginations
- **Have fun!**

Weekday opportunities at all
five Fairfax County Park
Authority Nature Centers

Contact **Jane Doe** at **555-0000**
for information and an application.
Training provided.
Applications due by **August 31.**

printed on recycled paper

Courtesy Fairfax County Park Authority, Conservation Division, Fairfax, VA.

Photocopied onto recycled, light brown, 8 1/2" x 11" paper. Same artwork is also reduced to 50% for reproduction in newsletters as an "ad."

This simple bulletin board flyer conveys several themes. It is designed to attract adults who want to work with children, particularly in one of the Park Authority's historic sites. See how it speaks to past and future, roots, and being a role model to the young. It would be especially useful in places seniors are likely to see it. The flyer always shows a deadline date so that volunteers can apply in time for the next scheduled training session.

Even though this flyer violates my suggestion not to use the word "volunteer" as a headline, the word is balanced by other phrases and the artwork. Having the recycled paper logo fits the proper image of a conservation program and was included consciously for this purpose.

FRONT COVER

INSIDE SPREAD

Courtesy the Philadelphia Geriatric Center, Philadelphia, PA.

Printed on glossy, lightweight stock in burgundy, gray and black ink.

This is an example of a program brochure outlining what volunteers do at the Center and giving some information about the work of the Center itself. It has an upbeat, welcoming tone. It was carefully worded to be appealing. The photographs show diversity and tend to negate any stereotypes about a geriatric facility having only bedridden residents. Note the map on the back, helping prospective volunteers to locate the facility.

The brochure has an insert (usable with or without the wrap-around piece) targeted specifically at young/ student volunteers. Note the vocabulary choice of "Great Explorations!" and "Good Vibrations!" for that age group.

FRONT

BACK

Life is like a ten speed bike....

Most of us have gears we never use.

COVER

Courtesy Richfield Nursing Center, Salem, VA.

Printed on white card stock in aqua ink.

Compared to the carefully typeset and designed Philadelphia Geriatric Center brochure, this piece was clearly developed on a more limited budget. But it still works. The approach is clever and eye-catching.

Find your missing gear -

VOLUNTEER

NURSING UNIT/GROUP

MONTHLY BIRTHDAY PARTY VOLUNTEER

BEAUTY SHOP VOLUNTEER

ARTS AND CRAFT ASSISTANT

TRANSPORTATION AIDE

IMPPROMPTU VISITATION

ONE ON ONE VISITATION

THE SUNSHINE CART

FISHING HELPER

DAYROOM ATTENDANT

TAKE RESIDENTS OUTSIDE

READ

WRITE LETTERS

TAKE RESIDENTS TO ACTIVITIES

HELP DELIVER MAIL

DELIVER SNACKS

PLAY TABLE GAMES

HELP AT LARGE EVENTS, COOKOUTS
PARTIES, ENTERTAINMENT

Richfield Nursing Center

The finest medical and nursing care in an atmosphere of love and understanding.

Richfield Nursing Center provides skilled, intermediate and extended care to senior citizens in an environment that is uniquely rich in recreational opportunities and social interaction. The goal is to nurture the mental, physical, and spiritual well-being of every resident.

We are licensed by the Virginia State Board of Health, and certified by the federal Department of Health and Human Services for Medicare, Medicaid, and other federal health programs.

Constructed to ensure the safety of each resident, Richfield Nursing Center is equipped with smoke detectors, automatic sprinkler systems, fire alarms, and secure care system (for wandering patients).

Residents feel right at home in the clean, comfortable surroundings of our modern private and semiprivate rooms. Each room features air conditioning, adjustable beds, spacious closets, safety-equipped bathrooms, and bedside electronic call buttons for round-the-clock nursing care.

Restoring patients to their maximum level of self-care is the goal of the fully equipped facilities of the Physical Therapy Department.

Tear here and return to Richfield

Volunteer Coordinator
Richfield Nursing Center
1000 Main Street
Anytown, U.S.A.
555-0000

I AM INTERESTED IN BECOMING A VOLUNTEER.

NAME _____

ADDRESS _____

CITY _____ STATE _____ ZIP CODE _____

GROUP NAME: _____ TELEPHONE # _____

SPECIAL TALENTS: _____

INSIDE SPREAD

What's a little time between friends?

Share a moment, be a friend.

friendly
♥*isitor*

POSTER 1

Be a friend.

By placing a simple phone call to the Friendly Visitor Service of the Southwest Christian Ministry, you can help someone who may need a friend.

Share a moment, be a friend.

friendly
♥*isitor*

POSTER 2

Share a moment

Do you remember a time when you needed a friend, but no one was with you? You reached for the phone or paid a visit, because you hated that feeling of loneliness.

In Reading there are many elderly people who never escape from that feeling. They're white, black, Hispanic, single, or isolated with a spouse. They live in the city and can't get out much. Even if they do have a family nearby, their family can't sit all of the time. They need a friend. Not a nurse, or a chauffeur, or a servant. Just a friend who'll share a few minutes with them.

We are your neighbors of the Southwest Christian Ministry's Friendly Visitor Program, and we want you to join us in helping these people. We'd like you to consider becoming a friend to a lonely elderly person or couple living near to you.

...Be a friend.

The Friendly Visitor Program is a simple way for one human being to bring companionship into the life of another human being who needs it. As a volunteer, you'll share some laughter, pay a visit, or make a phone call. You might grocery shop for your elderly friend, or write a letter to a grandchild, or just sit and talk for a few minutes a week. You won't be asked to provide special services or skills . . . just to open your circle of friendship and let

someone in. Southwest Christian Ministry will provide orientation, and you'll always be able to call on us for support and guidance.

Give and receive.

We think you'll get as much out of the Program as you pour into it. Ask one of our Friendly Visitors, and they'll tell you that this is an involvement your whole family can share, working together to tell someone that "we care." They'll tell you that visiting an elderly person will ease your mind from your own concerns and into someone else's, so you'll both feel better. And they'll tell you that the Program can be a real joy, because no matter how successful or involved you may be, it's always a pleasure to make a new friend. Call us at ▇▇▇▇ and let us know if you can be a friend. ▇▇▇▇

friendly
♥*isitor*

Share a moment, be a friend.

Courtesy Reading Urban Ministry, Reading, PA.

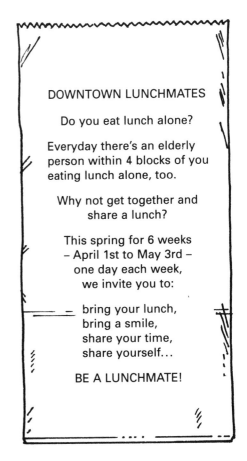

DOWNTOWN LUNCHMATES

Do you eat lunch alone?

Everyday there's an elderly person within 4 blocks of you eating lunch alone, too.

Why not get together and share a lunch?

This spring for 6 weeks
– April 1st to May 3rd –
one day each week,
we invite you to:

bring your lunch,
bring a smile,
share your time,
share yourself...

BE A LUNCHMATE!

Courtesy Reading Urban Ministry, Reading, PA.

Posters and brochure printed on textured cream-colored heavy stock in brown and red ink. Posters are 17" x 22". Brochure measures 3 1/2" x 5 1/2" when folded. Brown paper bag measures 3 1/2" x 6 3/4" when flat and is printed in red ink.

This was a complete *campaign* to find friendly visitors for homebound elderly people, targeted specifically at *church congregation members*. The campaign went as follows:

In the beginning, each church received Poster 1, asking "What's a little time between friends?" to hang in its vestibule. At the same time, the small brochure was distributed to each church in bulk quantity. Please note that the *size* of the brochure was carefully selected to fit into the literature racks in the vestibule!

In the second month, the poster was changed to Poster 2: "Be a Friend." Of course, the clergy were also asked to refer to the volunteer recruitment campaign in sermons and at other times.

Finally, the "brown bag" piece was cleverly used in non-church, public places such as a park to catch the attention of *people eating lunch* (a great target audience) near the homes of possible elderly "matches."

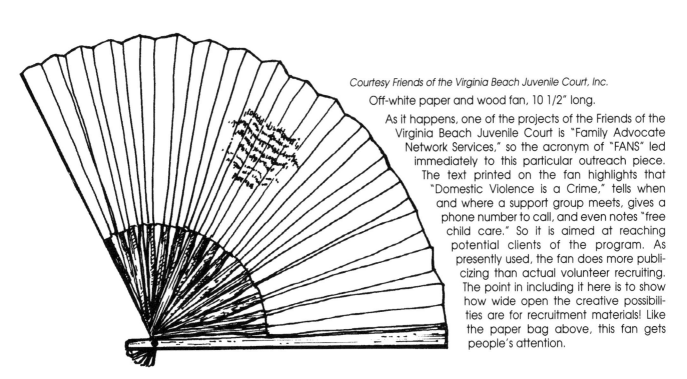

Courtesy Friends of the Virginia Beach Juvenile Court, Inc.

Off-white paper and wood fan, 10 1/2" long.

As it happens, one of the projects of the Friends of the Virginia Beach Juvenile Court is "Family Advocate Network Services," so the acronym of "FANS" led immediately to this particular outreach piece. The text printed on the fan highlights that "Domestic Violence is a Crime," tells when and where a support group meets, gives a phone number to call, and even notes "free child care." So it is aimed at reaching potential clients of the program. As presently used, the fan does more publicizing than actual volunteer recruiting. The point in including it here is to show how wide open the creative possibilities are for recruitment materials! Like the paper bag above, this fan gets people's attention.

GIVE US A BREAK
AND WE'LL GIVE YOU ONE, TOO

You are invited to Rohm and Haas's first Volunteer Fair on Thursday, November 13th. The Volunteer Fair will be held in the new Home Office cafeteria, the Hearth, from 2:30 P.M. to 4:00 P.M.

A Volunteer Fair is a gathering of local nonprofit agencies and organizations, a chance for you to meet groups like the Girl Scouts, the Center for Literacy, the Academy of Natural Sciences, and the Balch Institute. Rohm and Haas has invited 25 such groups to the Home Office on November 13th to tell you about their work, how they help out in the community, and why they need volunteers — like you.

Visit the fair and hear what these groups have to say. Enjoy the free cider, ginger snaps, coffee and tea, and learn about these agencies and their community work. You don't have to volunteer, but you may find you'll want to.

Remember to mark it on your calendar:

The First Rohm and Haas Volunteer Fair
Thursday, November 13th
In the Hearth
2:30 P.M. to 4 P.M.

This program is sponsored by the Rohm and Haas Corporate Social Investment/Community Affairs Department as a service to employees and the communities of the Delaware Valley.

Courtesy Rohm and Haas, Philadelphia, PA.

Photocopied on 8 1/2" x 11" white paper.

This was a bulletin board flyer used to announce the company's on-site Volunteer Fair. The headline, "Give Us a Break...," fits the audience perfectly: employees who must choose to attend the Fair during their afternoon break time.

What Would it Take to Persuade You…

(INSIDE)

…*to Join the Friends of the Clark*

Courtesy Sterling and Francine Clark Art Institute, Williamstown, MA. Brochure designed by Kate Emlen.

Printed on white card stock, 4" x 9". Multi-color reproduction of the painting, *Nymphs and Satyr* by Bouguereau.

This piece works precisely because it is aimed at art lovers. If a different type of organization had used the same graphic, it might have seemed "cutesy." Here it humorously and appropriately plays on the cultural sensibilities of the primary audience who may well already be familiar with the painting—and now see it in a new light. The brochure's tone is lovely.

The interior text of this brochure focuses on paying an annual fee in exchange for basic museum benefits. This is the main purpose of Friends of the Clark. As we will discuss in Chapter 13, it is possible to use this type of brochure to say much more about the responsibilities of membership or the ways members can actively participate (volunteer, become an officer, etc.)—if your organization wants to give prospective members a sense from the beginning that there is more to being part of your group than just paying dues.

grow
learn
experience
give care
expand help
contribute
nurture
share teach
smile
Volunteer

Save your place with this while you serve your community as a volunteer. The Voluntary Action Center can help you find the place where your interests and skills are most needed, or where you can explore new areas of interest.

Call, write or visit
The Voluntary Action Center
1000 Main Street
Anytown, U.S.A.
555-0000

Courtesy the Voluntary Action Center of the St. Paul Area, MN.
Printed on cream-colored, textured card stock in deep red ink, 2 1/4" x 8 1/2".

Bookmarks are versatile, inexpensive recruitment tools. Even though they require a heavy card stock, you can obviously get eight to twelve bookmarks out of one sheet of paper. They can be placed in waiting rooms, at check-out counters (bookstores, libraries, gift shops), or anywhere people might want to pick up a practical, handy bookmark. These are especially ogical as a recruitment piece aimed at students or for finding tutors and instructors. This example was used by the Voluntary Action Center to increase the general public visibility of volunteering.

We need someone with the boldness of a pioneer, the resourcefulness of an inventor and the faith of a sword swallower.

We need someone to fill a unique job opening.

Someone to spend two years in another country. To live and work in another culture. To learn a new language and acquire new skills.

We need someone who wants to help improve other people's lives. Who's anxious to build lasting friendships. To gain memories and experience that will last a lifetime. And a sense of fulfillment few jobs can match.

We need a Peace Corps volunteer. Interested? The first step is easy. **Call us at 1-555-0000.**

Peace Corps.
The toughest job you'll ever love.

This ad was used in publications of all types. The headline is wonderful. It is cheerful and positive, yet successfully conveys the seriousness and intensity of the work to be done in the Peace Corps. I also like "the first step is easy" forewarning at the end.

Courtesy Community Service Volunteers, London, UK.

Printed on card stock in fuchsia, red, black and white. Folded size is 7 3/4" x 8 1/4".

This piece comes from the United Kingdom. It is recruiting candidates for full-time, demanding volunteer roles. The long-standing philosophy of CSV is that no applicant is ever turned down. The text inside the brochure helps the reader understand that CSV volunteer work is serious, as well as meaningful to both the recipient and the volunteer. The set of photos on the front is meant to grab attention and certainly the young man's expressions are not run-of-the-mill. The slogans "life experience doesn't take a lifetime" and "you'll be surprised by what you can give, *we won't*" are very affirming. CSV uses these as the headlines on other recruitment pieces.

You can help out anywhere. But you belong at the YMCA.

As a YMCA volunteer, your time and talent go a long way. You can lead a program, serve as a role model for young people, help out in the office or at a special event, raise money, or be part of a group or committee working on a neighborhood problem. No matter how you help, you'll make a big difference as you work with others to create a feeling of connectedness in your community.

To solve the problems closest to home—or better yet, to prevent them before they begin—the YMCA needs more people like you. Do something good. Volunteer at the YMCA. Please stop by or call for details.

You can help out anywhere.
But you belong at the YMCA.

As a YMCA volunteer, your time and talent go a long way. You can lead a program, serve as a role model for young people, help out in the office or at a special event, raise money, or be part of a group or committee working on a neighborhood problem. No matter how you help, you'll make a big difference as you work with others to create a feeling of connectedness in your community.

To solve the problems closest to home—or better yet, to prevent them before they begin—the YMCA needs more people like you. Do something good. Volunteer at the YMCA. Please stop by or call for details.

Reprinted with permission from The Seven Rs of Volunteer Development, copyright 1994, the YMCA of the USA, Chicago, IL.

The YMCA of the USA has provided a packet of nationally-designed volunteer recruitment materials for use by local affiliates. The packet contains "slicks" (camera-ready artwork on glossy paper—the best for reproduction purposes) such as the ones shown for reproduction in just about any type of publication (with local information inserted). Note that the text is the same on all the pieces, but the different shapes and sizes attract attention each time. The text is effective with and without photographs.

Doer's Profile

Space for photo

Name:

What do you do for the YMCA?

Why do you volunteer for the YMCA?

What do you do when you're not volunteering?

For you, there's nothing more fun than.....

Your philosophy of life in 25 words or less:

YMCA Volunteers
Do
SOMETHING
GOOD

Reprinted with permission from The Seven Rs of Volunteer Development, copyright 1994, the YMCA of the USA, Chicago, IL.

Templates (a pattern that can be used over and over) are also given to YMCA affiliates for a combination recognition/recruitment strategy: the "Doer's Profile." This type of poster usually gets attention. The Doer's Profiles are meant to be completed locally with real photos and biographic information, and then posted in the Y building or put in the local newspaper. The individual volunteers selected for the campaign will feel appreciated, and the public becomes informed about volunteering at the YMCA by relating to the profiled volunteer.

You can help out anywhere. But you belong at the YMCA.

As a YMCA volunteer, your time and talent go a long way. You can lead a program, serve as a role model for young people, help out in the office or at a special event, raise money, or be part of a group or committee working on a neighborhood problem. No matter how you help, you'll make a big difference as you work with others to create a feeling of connectedness in your community.

To solve the problems closest to home—or better yet, to prevent them before they begin—the YMCA needs more people like you. Do something good. Volunteer at the YMCA. Please stop by or call for details.

Do
SOMETHING
GOOD
Volunteer at the YMCA

This Summer
Pick On Someone
Smaller Than You Are

Phone United Way's
Volunteer Atlanta Summer Youth Program
555-0000

Courtesy Volunteer Resource Center, United Way of Metro Atlanta, GA.

Printed in black on white 8 1/2" x 11" paper.

This small poster was one of several in the campaign for teenage and college-age young people to be summer volunteers in Atlanta public playground programs. The posters all used this same provocative, play-on-words headline, but the photographs pictured different groups of children and volunteers. Care was taken to be multi-racial and to show everyone having fun. This example illustrates how "a picture is worth a thousand words" if an organization wants to attract young men as volunteers.

Inviting, Not Pleading

You have a set of volunteer job descriptions and have brainstormed where to look for the most qualified volunteer for each assignment. You have selected a recruiting technique from the previous two chapters to match the most likely sources. You are now ready to word your message.

Crafting Your Message

"We need help."

This is the common message of volunteer recruitment. Even more common is the implication:

"We need cheap help."

While this approach may grab some attention, it certainly does not differentiate you from a hundred other agencies in town—all under-staffed and over-demanded. The truth is, *everyone* needs help. Your job as a volunteer recruiter is to invite potential volunteers to *select* the opportunities in your organization that are the best match for them. Put another way, your message is:

"We are worth your time and effort. We offer you the opportunity to become involved with us so that we can utilize your talents and you can feel like you're making a real contribution."

A bit longer to convey subliminally, but much more successful! Note, too, that you are saying "we want you if we're right for each other" instead of "we'll take anyone if they'll work for free."

Whether you are recruiting in person or through written materials, the manner in which you present the invitation to become involved is very important. You are trying to strike a balance between providing enough information to interest a prospective volunteer and furnishing too much data that over-sells your case. You also want to sound welcoming to newcomers without implying that every applicant will be immediately accepted.

So, what should you say?

First, remember that your initial goal is to encourage people to express interest in volunteering with your organization. Once someone has applied, you can provide many more details about your setting and about the specific volunteer work assignment. At the recruitment stage, explain only the basics:

- Introduce your organization as succinctly and clearly as possible. What do you do? Whom do you serve? What have been your successes? And don't forget to include the vital facts such as where you are located.

- Explain how volunteers contribute to the work of the organization. What have volunteers achieved in the past? What kinds of people volunteer?

- Explain what work needs to be done and why a volunteer may be well suited to do it—go over the major elements of the volunteer job description.

Speak to your successes because people like to join in enterprises that accomplish something. Use your

93

data—how many clients have you helped? how many teenagers have you placed into jobs? etc. On the other hand, another appealing idea is to volunteer as part of a new venture. If yours is a pioneering effort, use that fact, too.

Helping People to Choose

Now you are ready to speak to the issues of greatest interest to the individuals weighing whether or not they might want to pursue a volunteer placement with you: what will be expected of a volunteer. You want candidates to do self-screening, whether they are reading your literature, hearing your speech, or facing you across the interview desk. As clearly—and *truthfully*—as possible, describe:

1. The tasks that need to be done: Is this a job requiring lots of creative thinking? Some physical labor? Has the work already been designed or will the volunteer participate in determining how the job is to be done?

2. The context of the work: What will be accomplished? Is the volunteer one of many filling the same assignment or is this a special job? Will the volunteer work alone or with others? Are there deadlines to meet? Are other projects occurring concurrently that will affect the volunteer assignment? How will the volunteer know that the work is successful?

3. Time considerations: How much time will this take weekly or monthly? What schedule would be best and is there room for flexibility in when the work has to be done?

   What are you hoping for as an initial commitment in terms of duration? Do not be afraid to request what you need! If this assignment really requires a minimum of six months, one year, or even more—*say so at the recruiting stage.*

Let me re-emphasize our recurring theme: your goal is to find the *best candidates* for your vacant volunteer assignments. Rather than making the work sound easy, it is much better to challenge prospects from the beginning. If someone does not apply because the job sounds too demanding, you have *succeeded* in screening out someone who would not have done the job anyway! Conversely,

the person who wants to learn more about the assignment even after hearing your full expectations is likely to be willing to *do* the work. Some people are more intrigued by something that sounds difficult than by something that sounds as though just anyone can do it.

It may be hard to accept that it is better to live with a vacancy than to compromise and put the wrong volunteer into that assignment—but it is true. You can always negotiate and possibly compromise much later in the game. But at the start, *ask for what you want*—no matter how demanding it may sound.

Back to our list . . .

4. Explain any possible out-of-pocket costs to the volunteer and what, if anything, will be reimbursed.

5. Highlight training that you offer. Remember our discussion about why people don't volunteer? Fear of failure and uncertainty about their ability to do the job are frequent concerns. Simply indicating that you *offer* training makes recruiting easier because it implies that you do not expect newcomers to arrive with full-blown skills.

6. Tell what qualifications or characteristics would be ideal.

7. Indicate the benefits (tangible and intangible) volunteers can expect in return for their service. Talk about the impact or result of the volunteer's effort on your cause or client group. But also point out how the volunteer will learn new things, gain new insights, etc.

As you consider what to include in your recruitment "pitch," you would be wise to *avoid* the following:

- *Speaking with forked tongue.*

   In our desire to get prospects to say yes, we may say what we think they want to hear, rather than what we really want of them. So we minimize the work to be done or the time needed to do it, or we gloss over the less glamorous parts of the job. We know that we aren't telling the "whole" truth, but we fudge a little to make volunteering sound

THE VOLUNTEER RECRUITMENT BOOK/ELLIS
INVITING, NOT PLEADING

more appealing. As I've already said, this is a self-defeating approach.

A thought to consider: If you find yourself unable to tell the truth about a volunteer position, diagnose why. Maybe your discomfort is an indicator that you should reconsider the assignment. Re-design the job or address the problem (is it a gravy stain?) and you'll soon discover honesty coming much easier.

- *Playing on guilt.*

This no-no is not as obvious as some of the others. It is evidenced by recruiting with messages such as "our need is greater than theirs" or "what have you done to help the less blessed lately?" You should not have to shame people into volunteering. This also tends to focus on *noblesse oblige*, in which people help more to make themselves feel better than to empower others.

- *Asking for a favor.*

It is not a good approach to plead: "Do me a favor and help with this." People should want to volunteer because the work itself is worthwhile, not to help *you* personally (spouses and children excepted!). This is strongly connected to playing on guilt.

A great point to consider: Recruiting is never asking people to do you a favor. Instead, you are **offering them an opportunity** to do something important and you don't want them to be left out!

Tone

Be welcoming in your tone. It is possible to convey the seriousness of the work to be done and still talk about the fun side of volunteering (the nice people, the camaraderie, etc.). Would someone *want* to join you? Will it be a good use of free (recreational) time?

Tone is conveyed in a number of ways. The style of the speaker is one—level of formality, use of humor, openness to questions, etc. Another element of tone is vocabulary—choose your use of jargon, complexity of sentences, or academic words carefully.

You are setting the stage for this volunteer's

ongoing interactions with your organization. So it is important to be motivated yourself. People are attracted to genuine enthusiasm.

Face-to-face Recruiting

If we accept the truism that a majority of people volunteer because they were "asked," then we should expect to do as much personal, one-to-one recruiting as possible. This means that once we have identified prospective candidates, we need to frame our individual conversations so that we are successful in issuing our invitation to volunteer.

Face-to-face recruitment offers people the opportunity to explore with you whether or not they fit into your organization. As I have said several times before, you have not failed as a recruiter if someone declines to volunteer with you. The decision to say no may be the right decision. For whatever reasons, this prospect may not meet your qualifications or your organization may not be best for this person.

The key is to make sure that a "no" is indeed based on a valid assessment, rather than on misconceptions. And even if this conversation does not lead to the person becoming a volunteer, you can still make a friend for your organization. People who have been approached to help can become supporters in many ways, from giving money to being community advocates. The process of recruitment is one of education. Each person who talks with you should come away with a good feeling about your organization, and with more information than s/he had before.

Many recruiters do fine in giving speeches or disseminating written materials, but freeze at the thought of direct confrontation with a recruit. The "ask" is hardest when it seems most intimate—or perhaps when possible rejection seems the most personal. It should help to recognize that such individual contact is *always positive*, even if the result is a no to the invitation to volunteer. Why? Because it is always *flattering* to ask someone to participate. You are implying, if not actually saying, that this person has talents that are wanted and needed. If you did not feel the person was a potentially good volunteer, you would not be having this conversation. As just discussed, you are not begging, or twisting anyone's arm, or asking someone to do you a favor. You are the bearer of a great *opportunity*—the chance to become involved in important, enjoyable work.

The major benefit of one-to-one conversation as a recruitment technique is that you can tailor your approach directly to the person in front of you. In addition to the details of the work, spend some time explaining why you think this person is a good candidate for this role. Why did you ask him or her? Was it her skills? His professional expertise? Her standing in the community? Did someone he respects recommend him? While flattering, this is not "flattery." There should be a good reason why you are asking this particular person to fill this particular volunteer position.

Your most important tools are *listening* and *observation*. Give the person a chance to ask questions and react to what you have said. Does s/he seem interested? What aspects of your presentation are getting the most attention?

Face-to-face recruiting is related to the skills of interviewing in that you need to ask good questions. There will be times, in fact, when you can combine recruiting and interviewing so that when you are done with the conversation, you have actually signed up a new volunteer. Some possible queries:

- *Tell me if anything in your background seems relevant to this assignment.*

- *Have you done any similar volunteer work before?*

- *Is there something you would like to learn (a new skill) through your volunteer work?*

- *Have you been concerned about the issues I've been describing?*

I want to clarify that I recommend using the person's skills or talents as a *conversation starter*. It may happen that this candidate is absolutely uninterested in doing volunteer work related to his or her job or other "credentials." S/he wants to do something fun and different as a volunteer. That's fine and you can work from there in your interview. But it still makes sense to *start* with what you know about the prospect.

Re-read the section on why people do not volunteer on pages 24 to 28. Be prepared to answer questions truthfully and to raise possible concerns

yourself rather than make the candidate feel awkward about having some fears. This is a balancing act, of course. You want to acknowledge that every opportunity carries some negatives without *introducing* problems that aren't bothering the prospective volunteer!

Negotiating

As you explain what you expect from a volunteer, watch the prospect's reactions. Let him or her raise questions or objections—don't jump the gun by changing your job description to elicit a nodding head. If the candidate does ask how flexible you can be, *consider carefully* before compromising! But . . . go ahead and negotiate *if* you really can adapt without losing the essence of the assignment.

If the person expresses an interest but wants to make too many changes to the stated job description, be prepared to offer other options for volunteering. Maybe another assignment altogether will be a better match.

If the candidate seems hesitant, but interested, suggest a way s/he can "test the water." Is there a one-time assignment that would allow him or her to be helpful while getting a feel for the way your organization works? This is why having a variety of job descriptions is so useful.

In the chapter on why people do and don't volunteer, we talked about the common turn-down of "I'm too busy." Sometimes this is a valid assessment of what is happening in the person's life at this moment. But it is also a convenient way to say no without having to acknowledge that your organization or the volunteer work itself is just not interesting enough to the candidate to "make time" to become involved.

When someone raises the issue of too little time, probe a bit more. Try a follow-up question, such as: "Would you prefer me to call back in a month?" or "Is there another type of volunteer assignment that you would prefer to do?" Another approach would be: "If you had the time, would this volunteer assignment interest you?" If the answer is yes, you might negotiate a return call in the future. If the answer is no, you can follow up with possible other ways the person can volunteer with your organization.

Don't Have Mental Conversations

One of the more self-defeating things recruiters do is have mental conversations with prospective volunteers. Most of these silent exchanges go something like this:

Recruiter: *"Gee, I'd love to have this person as a volunteer. But s/he is so busy . . . and s/he probably won't want to work on Saturdays . . . and s/he might feel this assignment isn't challenging enough . . . oh, I guess the answer will be no, so I won't even ask."*

Have you noticed the problems in the above conversation? First, it isn't a conversation at all, because it's one-sided. The prospect is not doing any talking—and, in fact, hasn't even been asked. Yet the conversation ends with a "no."

If you never ask the prospect, you cannot get a yes answer.

Since we have already decided that it is never insulting to ask someone to volunteer, give your prospect the courtesy of a *real* conversation. She or he might actually say *yes* and become the volunteer you most hoped to attract! If she or he says no, as you anticipated, you can still talk about other possible leads. Or, as we have been discussing, you might be able to negotiate a smaller amount of help—something is better than nothing.

If the Answer Really Is No

You will not succeed in recruiting everyone. But you can sometimes lay the foundation for future contacts, win a new financial donor, or gain a referral source. Thank the prospect for her or his consideration. Ask if s/he has any ideas as to where else you might look for a volunteer. Would s/he want to be kept on your organization's newsletter mailing list? As we have said before, make a friend.

Turning a Candidate Down

Let's not assume that you will always be running after reluctant prospects. Sometimes the tables will be turned and you will have an eager applicant about whom you have real reservations.

Good for you! There is no law that says every organization must accept every offer of help.

When you feel you have an inappropriate candidate, assess the reasons for your reaction. Is there a clear lack of qualifications or is there something less tangible that is making you cautious? Just as in the hiring of employees, the screening of volunteers is as much an art as a science. And all the techniques of personnel management work here, too. For example, ask for and contact references. Involve others in additional screening levels, asking candidates to participate in more than one interview.

Consider asking the person to come in for a one-time assignment as a test for you *both*. "If you help us on Saturday afternoon, we can become better acquainted and talk afterwards more specifically about whether volunteering here on an ongoing basis is right for you."

The subject of interviewing could fill another book, of course. For our purposes here, keep in mind that the information you exchange with an applicant is another stage of the recruiting process and that even now you want self-screening to occur, if necessary. It is vital, however, not to evade turning someone down by saying "we'll call you" and then not doing so.

The potential need to turn someone down is why it is so important to make it clear as you recruit that candidates must "apply." It is so much harder to screen someone out if you have implied that all comers will be accepted. If each applicant knows that there is a screening process, you can turn people away with neutral or even helpful statements such as:

— *"We are interviewing a number of people and need to find the most qualified."*

— *"There are only a limited number of openings."* (*If* this is true! Don't say this if you really need 100 people and must keep recruiting for the next two months!)

— *"Given my knowledge of our agency and this conversation, I am not sure we meet your needs—there is just not a good match here."*

— *"Your talents deserve a home with an organization that really needs these particular skills. Let me recommend that you keep hunting for the best volunteer assignment. Have you contacted the Volunteer Center? How about Agency X?"* (It is always good public relations to give people additional places to contact to continue their search for a volunteer role.)

If you must turn any applicants down, be clear about it. But you can still be supportive in their search for the right volunteer placement for them.

It is possible that you are in an agency that has decided never to turn away a volunteer, especially if the applicant is a program participant, resident, donor, or other stakeholder. Without debating the merits of such a rule, you are still under no obligation to assign any applicant to whatever specific volunteer job s/he wants. Just make sure you have a number of low-risk, low-people-contact assignments that can be used for volunteers who are not qualified for other positions. This should not be busy work—but also not a role that will undercut all the other qualified volunteers. (See pages 123-4 on participant-volunteers.)

In an ironic twist, if your organization develops the reputation of setting standards and not accepting every candidate who wishes to volunteer, you make being *accepted* as a volunteer a status symbol. This is a big boost to your ongoing recruitment efforts.

Reacting to Offers of Help

So far we have focused almost exclusively on a proactive approach to recruitment: you determine what you need and then find volunteers to match those needs. In real life, however, once you have begun to advertise your interest in finding volunteers, you will never know who might drop in out of the blue. How prepared are you to *react* if a prospective volunteer offers you a skill you didn't expect?

First, remaining true to our ethic of never wasting a volunteer's time, if you really and truly cannot find a way to utilize an offered skill, *refer the person elsewhere*! It is not our job to fit square pegs into round holes, nor to devalue someone's skill by ignoring it.

Reacting to an offer of help requires some creativity. Keep a "wish list" handy at your desk at all times. On it you record any statement you overhear that begins with: "I wish we had someone who could. . . ." Write down simple and complex tasks, sublime and ridiculous ideas. The list might include one-shot needs such as cleaning out the supply closet or taking old fundraising premiums to a flea market for sale, plus full-fledged projects such as developing a five-year marketing plan. The wish list can be very helpful when someone is at your desk with time and skills to give, but who does not seem to fit any established volunteer job description.

Sometimes you might not be sure if a person's skill area can be used well. You can tell the candidate that you will do some homework and let him or her know in a few days. Then you can approach staff members with a "flash bulletin": "Can you put this skill to good use? A prospective volunteer is offering us expertise in ＿＿＿ and can work X hours a week starting now. Please contact the volunteer office to discuss this further." Maybe you can stimulate some creative juices and end up with a great new volunteer job description—and a great new volunteer.

Pointers on Inviting People to Volunteer

- Be motivated yourself. Sincerity wins out over technique every time.

- Be clear on what you want people to do. Use written volunteer job descriptions whenever possible.

- Use titles. The word "volunteer" is a pay category, not a function!

- Be honest. Tell prospective volunteers what the work entails, even if you think it may sound like a lot. Avoid minimizing the work.

- Share deadlines up front. When does the work have to be finished?

- (Remember that it is better to live with a vacancy a little while longer than to convince the wrong person to become a volunteer.)

- Define the training and supervision or support the volunteer will have. This isn't sink or swim.

- Identify and express the benefits to the volunteer from accomplishing the task. The best volunteering is when the giver benefits as well as the recipient.

- Explain why you decided to ask this particular person to help—what skills or personality traits make him or her a good candidate for the position.

- It may be just as important to discover what a prospective volunteer wants to *learn* or *try* as a volunteer as it is to know his or her official credentials.

- Keep in mind that you can never insult people by asking them to volunteer. In fact, you are usually flattering them by implying that they have the talent to do the job.

- Paint an upbeat picture of the work. Volunteering should be fun.

- Hold the perspective that you are giving people the marvelous *opportunity* to participate in an important project. You don't want them to be left out!

- The best way to recruit volunteers is to *ask* people to help.

10
Doing It

In the "Steps to Successful Volunteer Recruitment" (pages 5-7), I include, as a specific task, the advice to *do it*. Once all is said and done, recruitment is an *activity*. Every element is important: good volunteer job design, consideration of where to look for candidates, selection of the right technique. But all of these take place at your desk. Only when you get out there and begin to issue your invitation—to *ask*—can you get results.

As a consultant, I am frequently requested to evaluate an organization's recruitment strategies. Before examining anything else, I ask for a list of where, specifically, recruitment messages have been disseminated over the last three months. If the volunteer program leader cannot name at least five distinct places in which active recruitment has been attempted, the primary problem is clear: volunteer recruitment must be *done,* not just considered.

Wishing for applicants, praying for them, or trying magic spells occasionally produces results—but these approaches leave a lot to Mother Nature. If you want more control over your volunteer recruitment outcomes, you have to expend a little effort.

The McDonald's Quotient

Over the past few years, I've begun to exhort trainees in my recruitment workshops to evaluate their recruitment efforts against what I have formulated as "The McDonald's Quotient." Simply put, the Quotient works something like this:

It seems to me fair to assume that 99% of North Americans know about and most even like McDonald's restaurants. This food store chain serves more meals in any given day than any other entity on the planet except for the U.S. Army (an interesting piece of trivia you are welcome to use at your next cocktail party).

Yet, in the past five or more years of my adult life, I cannot remember a *single day* in which I have *not* heard or seen *at least one* commercial for McDonald's. (So far, this observation has held true for every North American I have asked about his or her awareness of McDonald's advertising.)

So . . . if McDonald's feels that I have to be reminded, day after day, commercial by commercial, to consider buying its hamburgers, maybe (just maybe) a local volunteer program needs to put out its message about available volunteer opportunities more than once in awhile! And *that* is what I have come to call "The McDonald's Quotient."

Never assume "everyone knows" about you, even if you represent a traditional and well-known agency such as the Girl Scouts or the symphony orchestra or the municipal hospital. And if you represent an organization that is less recognized to start with (see Chapter 4 on image), it is even more foolhardy to think that occasional publicity and periodic recruitment messages are enough contact to make people remember you.

If you gave a speech to a civic club last spring, what can you do to remind them about you this fall? If you registered your agency with the local community college student volunteer office when they sent you their questionnaire last summer, can you revitalize that contact before the students leave for winter break? Are you certain that the bulletin board poster you placed in the senior center last month is still up?

Recruitment is a constant, year-round process of keeping your organization's name and its available volunteer opportunities in front of people. Consider some of the reasons why repetition makes sense:

- *Competition of messages.* Dozens, maybe even hundreds, of notices, announcements, and invitations bombard people all the time. This is true at home, at the work place, and at recreational venues. Some is what we call "junk mail," but much is valid and even appealing information—all hoping for some action from the recipient/listener/reader. "Do this," "buy this," "contribute money to this"—the demands go on and on. How can your message about volunteering compete . . . and be remembered?

- *Competition for volunteers.* Many organizations are seeking volunteers and most are worthy causes. What makes your message about openings in your setting more memorable or appealing?

- *Readiness of the prospect.* In order to recruit someone as a volunteer, the opportunity has to be a match not only between your organization's and the person's skills or interests, but also with his or her *availability.* If your recruitment message arrives at a bad time for the individual, the answer—at that moment—will have to be "no." But had your message been delivered six months earlier or a year later, that same candidate may well have become an active volunteer. Repetition of the invitation acknowledges the importance of timing.

- *Changing audiences.* We live in a mobile society. The people who heard your presentation two years ago are probably no longer members of that group and have been replaced by new folks—who have not heard your presentation. For ENERGIZE, this is proven over and over by our mailing list. Whenever we target a special mailing at folks we have coded as customers (those who have bought books from us in the past), we always include some older titles along with the new. Why? Because every time we market to past buyers, we discover that some customers have changed jobs and that their replacements have never seen a catalog from us. The agencies stay the same but the personnel move around. So even when we think we are speaking to old friends, we end up finding new ones. This applies to any outreach effort, including volunteer recruitment.

- *The general value of repetition.* Advertising experts are fond of saying that they know one-half of all advertising dollars are wasted; now, if they only knew which half . . . ! Another advertising truism is that it takes at least *three* contacts to make an impact. Sure some people respond immediately to the first ad, but most people are only subliminally aware of the first message sent. Only after repetition will someone be moved to *action* (and remember that advertising is about buying, just as recruitment is about volunteering). Repetition also implies credibility and stability, in that multiple messages reflect the staying power of a product (in this case, your organization). It isn't "fly-by-night"; it has continuity over time.

Maintaining a steady flow of recruitment messages throughout the year makes sense on every level. It also recognizes that no one recruitment strategy alone will be enough to fill all your needs. But the cumulative effect of consistent outreach should produce a steady flow of applicants because you have sown so many seeds in so many ways. Veteran recruiters will tell stories of new volunteers coming in with flyers that were distributed long ago, often to a friend or relative who passed them along a circuitous path until they reached the candidate calling you today.

Seasonal Efforts

Although I recommend continuous recruitment outreach, most organizations have found that certain times of year produce more success than others. It should not surprise you to learn that September, January and May are often effective recruitment periods. North American culture tends to organize itself around the school calendar and even adults plan their lives in terms of fall, winter-spring, and summer. So prospective volunteers are most approachable as they establish their seasonal calendars.

This is not to say that you should not recruit at other times. But save your energy for launching new campaigns just as a new season begins. Conversely, do not expect too many applications in December before the holidays or in mid-summer when most folks are focused on playing. *Unless* your recruitment strategy revolves around these very events. Finding volunteers to do holiday-related volunteering can be accomplished even up to the last minute (in fact, some procrastinators find themselves searching in vain for a way to express charitable holiday spirit if they have waited too long). Similarly, inviting volunteers after Memorial Day to "do good while having fun this summer" may work to your advantage.

In some cases, the timing of your recruitment campaign can purposely work "against type." A political organizer I know tired of being turned down by volunteers to do election day tasks such as poll watching. Because he usually recruited help in October for election day, he could not argue with people who said: "Gee, I'm sorry, but I won't have time on November X for anything except voting myself." So he hit upon the idea of calling people in *May,* after the primaries, for November election day work. The people he called were surprised to be asked so early but he effectively eliminated the excuse of "I'm booked that day." Instead, he elicited more honest responses such as: "I hate poll watching!" To such folks he could offer alternative political volunteer work, sometimes over the summer. But for those who said: "Sure, I'll help in November," he knew that he had placed himself on their calendars and they now needed reminders instead of last-minute recruitment.

Who Should Recruit

Recruitment is, as we have repeated often here, an ongoing process of welcoming the involvement of volunteers. Therefore, *everyone* in your organization shares an equal responsibility for recruitment. The director of volunteers or leader of the volunteer committee needs to develop outreach strategies, design recruitment materials, and coordinate formal recruitment efforts. But the issuing of individual invitations to apply for volunteer work can be—and should be—done by every employee and volunteer already on board.

It is impossible for one person to make contacts in every site in a community. You therefore need the help of everyone to make sure that your recruitment message is spread as widely as possible. Here's how:

1. Start with your executive director or president. Discuss how s/he can participate in the volunteer recruitment effort . . . and then require everyone else to follow suit. The top administrator should carry volunteer recruitment materials everywhere s/he speaks or has a meeting, requesting that these materials be posted or distributed. (You can work with the administrator to create targeted flyers or handouts for each site.) Note that it is important for you to know where such materials have been left, both so that you can follow up and so that you can avoid duplication in your own recruitment efforts.

2. Analyze brochures, newsletters, donor prospect literature, annual reports, and other materials used to describe your organization. Are volunteers mentioned? Substantively or superficially? If there are ways to incorporate more information about volunteers into agency publications, do so.

3. As we have already discussed, identify "missed opportunities" within your agency. Where can messages about volunteer openings be advertised to clients, visitors, and staff? Can you set aside a public bulletin board for information about volunteers (useful for recognition as well as for recruitment)? Is there recruitment material in the reception area? Are clients given vol-

unteer opportunity information at exit interviews? Are financial donors told about ways they can share their skills, too?

4. What is the Board of Directors doing to recruit volunteers? At least annually the board should be asked to identify places and ways to spread the word about volunteer openings. For example, if there is a corporate executive on the board, can you get an article in his or her company's in-house newsletter? Can the clergyperson on the board arrange for you to speak to some religious education classes?

5. Who else on staff has a job that requires community contacts? Again, anyone visiting local settings should be helping to disseminate literature about the volunteer program and mentioning the involvement of volunteers in oral presentations.

Note: for each of these representatives to be of most help, you need to keep them *informed* about specific, current volunteer openings and *supplied* with updated materials. They are not going to do your job for you. But it is their job to *help the agency* by spreading the word about volunteers.

6. Current volunteers can be great recruiters, as we have already discussed. But you need to ask them to recruit, and remind them to do so. Give them goals, deadlines, rewards, and *tools.* As already suggested, run an open house so they can invite their friends in or ask them to bring a non-related guest to the recognition event. At the very least, use the creative thinking of active volunteers by engaging them in planning sessions to brainstorm new sources of prospective volunteers, or new ways to reach them.

7. Current and past clients can be volunteer recruiters, too. As we discussed in the section on spheres of influence (page 52), satisfied customers have relatives and friends who might be interested in supporting you . . . but they may not be aware that you want them as volunteers.

In large volunteer programs needing to recruit many volunteers year round, it is common to designate one staff position as "Recruiter." While giving the Recruiter the main responsibility for outreach makes sense in terms of division of labor,

be careful that this person does not end up divorced from the rest of the volunteer program. It is very hard to invite people to volunteer without a strong understanding of the placement process and what is happening in the organization at any given time. Also, the Recruiter needs to be involved in volunteer job design, since this is so closely tied to appealing to various target audiences. Conversely, the danger of having someone assigned to recruitment is that other volunteer program staff may no longer feel it is their job to seek volunteers. Not so! Even with a full-time Recruiter, the work of keeping the public informed about volunteer opportunities benefits from the attention of as many people as possible.

Perhaps a better option (though less common) would be to rotate responsibility for recruitment—allowing each volunteer program staff member several weeks a year to focus solely on recruitment and then to return to his or her regular tasks. This would share the effort, keep everyone fresh, and make sure that any "recruiter" is closely connected to the day-to-day work volunteers will be doing.

Sincerity versus Technique

For all recruitment techniques requiring personal contact, the choice of who does the recruiting matters a lot. Like it or not, there is a level of charisma involved in successfully motivating people to volunteer. Prospective volunteers will respond more to a spokesperson who seems warm, likeable, and enthusiastic than to someone going through the motions of giving information. So the most important qualification for becoming a recruiter is the ability to convey genuine commitment: as I have said before, sincerity wins out over technique every time.

This establishes something of an ethical dilemma for you as a recruiter. The people you motivate to apply as volunteers are judging your organization by the tone *you* set. You serve as a representative of your setting. Therefore, if in your heart of hearts you feel that, back home, most staff are uncaring about volunteers and will be difficult to work with, are you misleading recruits? After all, it is your reputation on the line. People are applying because they believed *your* message. This is another reason why it is so hard to recruit until the proper preparation is done first.

Matching the Audience

Two questions often posed are: 1) Can a paid staff member be an effective recruiter of volunteers?; and 2) Can a person recruit volunteers who are different from him or her in terms of race, age, or other characteristics?

Some paid staff feel a degree of discomfort in asking other people to work for no pay while they themselves receive a salary. For the most part, this is more of a problem in the mind of the employee than in the minds of prospective volunteers and it is based on lack of understanding of what motivates people to volunteer. The fear of being confronted about some sort of double standard tends to make a recruiter apologetic from the start ("Gee, I know that I get paid and you won't, but please listen to my plea anyway. . . .").

While occasionally a person may remark on the perceived unfairness of paying some workers but asking others to be volunteers, the right candidate probably will not even think of such an objection. In most cases, it is obvious that the employee gives forty hours, fifty-two weeks a year to the cause, while the volunteer is going to provide much less time. In other words, for the employee the work is truly a job or career, while for the volunteer the work is an important contribution apart from what s/he might do to earn a living. Also, if the recruitment message is well designed, it will include an explanation of how volunteers add unique abilities to the work of the paid staff (see pages 5-6).

Recruiting for diversity is less clear cut. Certainly having recruiters who look like the target audience in color, gender, age, or other characteristic sets a tone of inclusion. But is it necessary to have a man recruit men or an African-American recruit other African-Americans? Is a woman or a white person doomed to failure in such an effort? I say no.

Remember my axiom about sincerity. It is offensive, and perhaps proves that you do engage in stereotyping, to assume that a listener will judge a recruiter only by his or her external appearance. Each recruiter should be genuine in his or her appeal to the audience and needs to appear *comfortable.*

Don't try to be something you are not. Most especially do not try to use vocabulary or jargon with which you are not familiar. If you are middle-aged, no amount of references to the slang current on MTV will convince a group of teenagers that you are "one of them"—and they don't want you to be! Dress for any group as you would to represent your organization, not to appeal to this group. At the very least, never "dress down." Be yourself. And if you sincerely feel welcoming to all types of people, that is the message you will send. If, on the other hand, you are unsure of how this audience will be received in your agency, or you feel uncomfortable or unsafe, don't make the presentation! Find another recruiter or pair up with someone who is more comfortable.

As we will discuss in Chapter 11 on diversity, the key is to design work relevant to any target audience. Show that they will not be tokens, but acknowledge if this is new outreach.

Being Ready

The fastest way to undercut a recruitment effort is lack of preparation for results! Do not schedule a vacation one week after a media appearance. Do keep your calendar free for interviews with recruits. Nothing is a bigger turn-off than hearing: "thanks for responding to our call for volunteers, but the first time we can see you is next month."

It is a big step for someone to pick up the phone to offer him/herself as a potential volunteer. In fact, this is the *riskiest* part of the recruitment process because the person is acting on initial motivation and is making him/herself vulnerable to the unknowns of your organization.

So who is the most important link in the recruitment chain? **The person in your organization who answers the phone!** Now picture who that is. How does s/he sound on the phone in general? Is this a pleasant voice, helpful to all callers? Or is this a perfunctory, even abrupt gatekeeper who makes callers of any kind feel like intruders? And what if your organization has moved to a voice mail system?!

Developing a plan for nurturing prospective

volunteers *the first time* they telephone (or walk in) is an absolutely critical element of your recruitment plan. If you have to deal with the Receptionist from Hell, this will be a challenge.

I have learned something interesting over the years. In most organizations, the switchboard or the reception desk is the first to field questions from the public, but the last to be informed about what is happening in the agency! No wonder receptionists become resentful.

When you launch a recruitment effort, take the time to go (in person) and visit with the receptionist, the switchboard operator, the guard at the door, and anyone else who is on the front line of dealing with the public. Show them samples of your recruiting flyers and explain the places you are reaching out for volunteers. Stress how important a warm first contact is to success in recruitment—and therefore acknowledge what an important part of your team this employee is. I promise you that this will work wonders! Once these staff members feel recognized and informed, they will understand their role. What you want them to do is:

- Be pleasant at all times. (Everyone in the organization will thank you for assuring that.)
- When someone identifies him/herself as seeking volunteer work, say: "Thank you for your interest in volunteering here."
- Never say: "the volunteer director isn't in; call back." Instead, say: "the volunteer director isn't in right now, but if you'll give me your name and number I assure you that I'll pass along the message and you'll hear from him/her as soon as possible."

Keep in mind that this mini-training session may have to be conducted with more people than receptionists and operators. In a small agency, the person taking messages for you may be another professional worker at the next desk who doesn't see him/herself as a "secretary." Again, explaining why it is important to take messages in a welcoming way will make a lot of difference.

(Parenthetical but important note: This is one of the reasons why the volunteer office needs a secretary!)

The Phone in Your Office

Now I want to comment on an unmentionable. In many settings, the volunteer office relies on volunteers themselves to answer the phone. All too often, it seems as though the least competent volunteers are kept to work in the volunteer office! I am truly tired of trying to call a colleague and getting someone (often aged or very young) who has absolutely no telephone skills at all—no courtesy or friendliness, and seemingly no ability to take a message accurately. And then they commit the worst sin of all. When asked something like, "do you know when the director is coming back to the office?" responds with, "well, I'm just a volunteer here." Is *that* what being a volunteer with your organization means?

The person (paid or not) who answers your phone represents the entire volunteer corps. If a brand new prospect is confronted with incompetence and confusion, why would s/he want to become a volunteer? Screen for those volunteers already skilled in answering the telephone and take the time to *train* them to do it the way you need it to be done. Consider this a factor in your recruitment campaign.

I further recommend that you test the system by calling in yourself and seeing what happens. Or get a "spy" to make the call for you—ask several friends or colleagues to phone, some who sound old, or young, or whatever.

Another related problem is the ubiquitousness of answering machines or voice mail. For after-hours messages or when all lines are busy, such electronic devices are wonderful. But I'll admit my prejudice that such impersonal systems can never substitute adequately for a welcoming human being. Whenever possible, try for the personal touch and have someone answer the volunteer office phone live. Failing this, be sure to record a friendly and informative message—and always return calls promptly!

SECTION III:

VARIATION

The chapters in Section III discuss the special challenges of reaching out to the widest possible audiences to find the best volunteers. Distinctive recruitment issues relevant to all-volunteer groups are covered in Chapter 13.

The Quest for Diversity

Some organizations are now seeking diversity but have not been open to differences in the past. They are trying to rectify years of being oriented to one gender or one age group or one social class. It is as difficult to introduce diversity into a volunteer program after the fact as it is to do so in any other aspect of our society, but it can be done.

Because our society is comprised of such a great variety of people, it is appropriate for organizations to reflect that mix. In general, the more varied our constituents, the stronger our base of support in the community and the better we are at serving our consumers. I say "in general," because some groups are homogeneous by design. A self-help group of nursing mothers has a defined membership. The Lithuanian Ancestors League also has a limited pool of participants. But most of us are in organizations attempting to provide services "to the community." If that is what we are about, then our service providers (employees and volunteers) should represent the diversity of our population.

"Diversity" has a simple definition and many connotations. It means that those who participate have a wide range of characteristics. However, in common usage, "diversity" has come to imply racial or ethnic integration. Ironically, the use of the word diversity has increased as the concept of "integration" has lost popularity. Integration has come to mean a *blending* of characteristics, inviting people from varied backgrounds to work together in similar ways toward common goals. For some, this approach has the danger of loss of identity to the stronger group. Instead, the current promotion of "diversity" encourages people from assorted backgrounds and mutual goals to find compatible but not necessarily identical ways to work together.

What this means is that if you sincerely want to open your doors to many types of people, you have to be willing to adapt. Diversity is not achieved if you are doing business as usual, but your participants only "look" different. True diversity includes being open to optional ways of conducting business.

What Does Diversity Mean to You?

Despite the frequent use of the word diversity to mean multi-racial representation, each organization will have a different need to expand its circle. Consider who is in the majority in your group. Here are some of the characteristics that might only be represented by a narrow band of choices:

- race
- gender
- age
- ethnic or national background
- language spoken
- income level
- education
- professions or job settings
- community power and influence
- political leanings

- religious beliefs
- sexual orientation
- physical disabilities
- geography: where people live or work
- degree of personal experience with your issue
- having ever been a client
- having ever been a donor or funder
- skills
- years with the organization

Analyze your paid staff, your clients, and current volunteers. After you have analyzed who your participants are now, ask: Is this the diversity we want or need?

It is also important to be informed about the demographics of your community. Who lives in your town? What is the mix of ages, races, etc.? Then you can ask: Are we representative of the local population? Are the employees and volunteers representative of our consumers or clients?

Be careful not to misuse the word "minority." Like the word diversity, minority has a dictionary and a popular definition. Its denotation is purely numerical: a minority is less than half of a group. But its connotation involves a comparison to who is in power: minorities are those who are different from those who control a group, an agency, a government. This is why women—who make up more than 50% of the United States population—are considered an under-represented constituency.

For the purposes of this book, who is in the minority (or majority) and who will "diversify" *your* organization are *relative* issues. A hospital auxiliary may need to recruit more men, a tutoring program may want more Spanish speakers, a senior center may want more participation from younger retirees in their sixties. It is up to you.

Causes of Lack of Diversity

There are many reasons why organizations are homogeneous. We have already noted that some are created that way by their mission. But most evolve into "sameness" over time. And then the hard part is changing the culture and recruiting different types of people once a tradition has been set.

As with other issues, you need to diagnose why there is a lack of diversity in your group. Some possibilities:

- For a long time there has been no outreach to anyone other than the immediate circle of current members. In other words, no one different has been asked to join.

- The desire for diversity has been publicized, but the deck is stacked. Much like the gravy stain parable, some organizations make it very difficult for someone to participate unless that person can comply with the many peripheral requirements. For example, if all meetings are held on weekday mornings, it may be hard to recruit people who are at a job at that time. This reinforces the message that only retired people need apply.

- The paid staff (and maybe the board) is homogeneous and prospective volunteers can see that money and authority are not being truly shared even though an effort is made to recruit different types of volunteers.

- Current volunteers are not at all welcoming of newcomers, especially if they are different in some way. Only a few leaders are pushing for diversity; the general membership undercuts the process.

- Your image in the community is so fixed that most people assume you want the volunteers you have and aren't really looking for other types of volunteers. They are surprised at your new recruitment outreach.

- The few "different" volunteers you have had in the past were tokens of your political correctness. They therefore felt isolated and merely tolerated. This type of experience is not conducive to people asking their friends to join up, too.

- The way that your organization has articulated its mission, defined community problems, or developed services is rooted in one—perhaps limited or ethno-centric—perspective. People with different perspectives (and alternate solutions) therefore do not feel mutual ownership of your work.

These are quite serious issues. Ultimately, it is foolish to consider diversity a "recruitment" problem if it is really an institutional prejudice problem. So you must address the root causes first.

It is this type of resistance to change that has led corporate America into workshops on human relations, multicultural diversity, and dealing with change. For many institutions, becoming truly open to diversity requires a major *culture shift*. If this is true of your organization, you may also have to begin with self-education before trying to recruit new volunteers. Otherwise, your recruitment efforts will be useless—the new volunteers will feel unwelcome or will recognize that they are tokens, and they'll leave.

You cannot transform the prejudices of every individual nor make each person warm and loving. But you can work toward removing barriers of rules and procedures, and you can support those participants who sincerely want to welcome a much more varied pool of volunteers.

It is certainly possible that there is no serious resistance to diversity lurking in your organization. In that case, you can focus your attention on the two subjects most important to successful recruitment: volunteer job design and outreach efforts.

Job Design That Welcomes Difference

As already implied, some organizations have unconsciously limited their appeal to a wider range of volunteers by their work traditions. Examine what you are asking volunteers to do and candidly assess if the tasks themselves have limited appeal (seeming perhaps too "female" or not "young" enough). Or maybe the titles that you have assigned to volunteer positions imply something you don't necessarily mean. It may seem incredibly obvious in retrospect, but I once was asked by a workshop participant how she could recruit more male volunteers. I asked her what assignments were vacant and she said, "Hostess." Honest. In the same vein, if all volunteer positions are called "Aides," you cannot expect corporate managers to picture themselves in such roles.

Revisit the earlier chapter on volunteer job de-sign to consider the interconnection of what you ask people to do and who may want to do it. The very structure of how things get done can send a message of exclusion: the time meetings are held, the expectation of having a car or tools like a computer, the degree of literacy required, the way people dress.

Examine these and other assumptions about volunteer work in your organization. Which factors cannot be changed because they are the most effective in accomplishing goals? Which are irrelevant to productivity and simply evolved over the years because past volunteers were comfortable this way? Are there other ways of doing things that might also work?

Do not presuppose that you have to make changes to diversify! This may actually be a negative stereotype. If you hope to attract more African-Americans, for example, it is insulting to act as if this group of citizens are all low income or under-educated. A teacher or lawyer who happens to be black will be able to handle the same type of volunteer job description as any other teacher or lawyer regardless of race. There may be other issues that make the African-American volunteer feel welcome or not, but the work design may be fine.

On the other hand, to attract some new groups you may well have to be more flexible. Unless you hold orientations in the evening, most day-time employees will be shut out of volunteering with you. Unless you let students change schedules each semester as their courses shift, you will lose them every three months. Unless you stop expecting committee chairpeople to host meetings in their homes (and provide refreshments), you may not draw working women to your cause. Conversely, selecting a neighborhood site for a training workshop demonstrates your interest in working with residents from that area.

Reaching out to new communities may require re-thinking some of the services your organization provides. Diverse volunteers may not agree with all of the methods used and may, in fact, have better ideas for how to solve problems. Is it feasible for your organization to consider making changes or to add (or at least test) alternative options? The answer to this question may be at the heart of your ability to attract new types of people to be volunteers.

Throwing Out the Rules

Up to now I have maintained the party line about defining volunteer work carefully, writing volunteer job descriptions, and maintaining some sort of structure. For most types of organizations, this is the best way to involve volunteers effectively—and not waste their time.

But there are other ways to be successful, too. Some settings or certain areas of work lend themselves to a much more relaxed, drop-in sort of approach that may attract a wider range of volunteers than anything else. For example, if you are doing a lot of outdoor work requiring many hands, why not send out the word that *anyone and everyone* who shows up on Saturday afternoons is welcome? Work team captains should be recruited with job descriptions, training, and some longer-term commitment, but each week their labor pool will expand and contract, and change. It is true that some weeks will see fewer volunteers than needed and other weeks more. But the goals of generating neighborhood enthusiasm, accomplishing a bit each week, and being welcoming to everyone can be met.

By actively spreading the message about the Saturday work crews to lots of different places (see next section on outreach), you will give new and possibly diverse groups of volunteers the chance to get to know you. Be sure to get people's names and addresses. Thank them later and share information about other ways volunteers can help out.

In Pittsburgh, a food pantry was having trouble recruiting volunteers willing to commit to a regular schedule of sorting and distributing donated food. So instead they allowed people to come in whenever they had the chance to serve a "shift." In order to make the new system work, all the pantry tasks had to be carefully reconsidered. A few were important enough to remain more formally defined and be assigned to key volunteers. But many of the tasks were "generalist" activities, doable by anyone who could follow instructions. Instruction sheets were therefore posted prominently and volunteers were asked to log in and out after a shift, noting what they had finished in their time on duty. I know of a clothing distribution center that did much the same thing.

The effect of this loosening up of structure is interesting. Some volunteers come in regularly while others are more unpredictable, some bring along family members and friends, some end up giving more time than before. On any given day, the work accomplished might be less than desired, but spread over a month, productivity is high. Most important for our focus here, all sorts of new volunteers can wander in, test the water, and test themselves in your setting.

Not every organization will have work conducive to this "throw out the rules" approach. But you may be surprised at what someone might be able to do to help if you are willing to loosen up. For example, can a volunteer bring a friend along one day even if that person has not applied or interviewed? For some jobs the best risk management answer has to be no. But for a lot of other work, the answer might be yes.

Do Active Outreach

Any public perception of your volunteer program as being closed to outsiders requires a vigorous campaign to counteract. Develop new job descriptions that appeal to as diverse a pool of prospective volunteers as possible and publicize these in places you have not yet been.

Do not rely on current volunteers to bring in more diversity. People tend to know only a few people who look and think like themselves. This is an excellent example of why it is limiting to ask: "Whom do we know who might want to do this?" The much better question is: "Whom *don't* we know who might want to do this?"

In your recruiting, *never* look for "some Asians" or "some teenagers with disabilities." That would be unconscionably bigoted. Why? Because seeking people only for their demographic data means that you care more about what they are on paper than about what they can contribute as volunteers. (Remember that we all define diversity outreach as finding people "other" than ourselves. We convey our exclusivity in all sorts of subliminal ways. For example, have you noticed the underlying assumption of this chapter yet? As aware as I want to be about inclusiveness, it is hard for me not to assume that most readers of this book will be white, middle class, or some other "majority" group member. So the examples I've used have mainly been about seeking volunteers who are not. But, of course, your diversity need may be to involve more white or middle class volunteers. Underlying assumptions affect our words and actions, which is why new audiences may react skeptically at first.)

Always approach recruitment as a search for talented individuals who meet real needs in your organization. Then as an added characteristic, you might also want a certain demographic profile. This means that you do the brainstorming exercise for "where can we find XXX skills" and then prioritize the list according to the rest of your profile wish list.

Let's go back to the list we brainstormed on page 46 for where to find drivers. Here it is again:

- car washes
- Traffic Court
- the Motor Vehicle Bureau
- drivers' education classes
- drive-in windows
- gas stations
- car showrooms
- taxi and bus depots
- truck stops
- drive-in movies
- car repair shops
- car accessory stores
- parking lots
- tire and parts stores
- car rallies
- car shows

If I need drivers to escort Hispanic and Latino clients to doctors' appointments, I now want to focus this list on sources with a better-than-even chance of having a bilingual population. (Note that I cannot assume that everyone who is ethnically Latino/Hispanic speaks Spanish, nor that everyone who speaks Spanish also speaks enough English to be a successful volunteer.)

If I do some research with Census data, I can identify Spanish-speaking neighborhoods. This means that if I go to a car wash or a drive-in bank window *in those neighborhoods,* I have a good

chance to communicate my message about volunteering to people who are *both* drivers and bilingual.

You can do the same exercise with any combination of skills and demographic characteristics. The goal is to place yourself where the majority of your audience fits the profile you are seeking. This marketing technique avoids a needle-in-the-haystack search and increases the chance of success.

The good news is that you may be able to use the exact same recruitment methods and materials already developed, but in new places. If your bulletin board poster seeking friendly visitors is hanging in the Native American Recreation Center, your desire to recruit Native Americans is strongly implied. Similarly, giving a speech to supporters of the United Negro College Fund or to the AIDS Self-Help Group carries the subtext of "we want you."

For other sources, however, you may need to redesign your materials to reflect your wish for diversity. Make sure photographs and slides show different ages, races, both sexes, etc. Bright colors may attract teenagers, more subdued colors may be more effective in reaching corporate executives. If and how you adapt will depend on whom you want to reach.

Get Help

If you are beginning a serious affirmative action campaign to recruit a large number of new volunteers, it may be extremely helpful to start by recruiting some advisors. Establish an Outreach Team or Diversity Task Force to generate recruiting ideas. Be honest about the changes you want to make in the volunteer corps. The desire for diversity will not come as a surprise to most people—but they may well need to be convinced of your sincerity. Tokenism will quickly be spotted. Real change will be supported.

While no one member of your Diversity Task Force can speak for his or her whole race, gender, or ethnic group, these volunteers can provide you with useful insights into what might turn candidates on or off to your organization. They certainly can give their perspectives on the questions of image and can help in brainstorming where to look for volunteers. Task force members can also open doors to new contacts and recruitment sources.

Another suggestion is to familiarize yourself with local publications that have audiences in various racial or ethnic communities. Not only will this increase your understanding of issues important to other groups, but you will undoubtedly find many leads useful in recruitment.

If you plan to recruit with foreign language materials, make certain these are written and reviewed by someone with a speaker's knowledge of this language—not a scholar's. Colloquialisms, tone, and double meanings need to be spotted (or used) or you run the risk of insulting prospective volunteers. Better to recruit in English well than in another language poorly.

More Outreach Ideas

Each ethnic community is different. One excellent resource for understanding the diversity within diverse populations is *Pass It On: Outreach to Minority Communities,* published by Big Brothers/Big Sisters of America (1992). The more you understand about the group you wish to attract, the better able you will be to frame an appealing message. Keep in mind that some recent immigrants may not be familiar with the concept of volunteering as we define it in North America. While charity and mutual aid are universal concepts, not every culture has organized forms of public volunteer activity. So your first outreach task might have to be introducing the *idea* of volunteerism. It is also important to know which institutions or community leaders have influence in certain neighborhoods and where the centers of activity are.

Here are a few tips:

- There are differences among the generation that was born elsewhere and immigrated here, and the first generation to be born here, and their children. Ethnic identity, bilingualism, and other national ties may weaken as generations assimilate.

- Never assume that racial or ethnic differences mean low income.

- Never assume that difficulty with English means lack of education or skills.

- Don't recruit in a foreign language unless the volunteer can work for you using that language. You are being misleading if you put out flyers in Korean but then expect all volunteers to speak English.

- If you are actively recruiting foreign-speaking volunteers, be prepared with someone on the phone who can handle non-English calls.

In the preceding chapter on "Doing It," we discussed the issue of whether or not a recruiter must "look like" the people s/he is trying to recruit. I believe that any sincere and prepared person can successfully recruit any prospect. See page 105.

Avoid Tokenism and Help Newcomers

Recognize that the first person to expand your group may feel a bit uncomfortable. Level with him or her about your sincere wish to increase the number of males, or teenagers, or African-Americans, and acknowledge that this new volunteer is a pioneer. If possible, recruit two to three new volunteers together and acknowledge that they are part of an outreach project. Let the newcomers be a support system for one another and advisors to you. Once they are working happily as volunteers, enlist their help in recruiting others.

One form of tokenism is to elevate the first "different" volunteer to the position of officer or leader without having earned that privilege. People know when they are asked to assume visible leadership roles as window dressing, rather than as recognition for real contributions made. Of course, you should also avoid the opposite extreme: maintaining the Old Guard in leadership roles long after new volunteers have done their time "in the trenches."

Because so many people volunteer for social as well as philanthropic reasons, try to mix newcomers and veterans in such a way as to get them better acquainted. Arrange some informal interaction time, even if it is only over a pre-work cup of coffee. Take care to introduce people with more than their names; share some information about each to get conversation started. If possible, send two volunteers out together to deliver or pick up

114

something, providing the chance to talk more personally.

A buddy system is an excellent approach to team building, providing there are clear tasks for the buddies to do together. Enlist veteran volunteers as orientation leaders and trainers. But also design group exercises that show the skills the newly-recruited volunteers bring to the organization. The various essays in *Managing Volunteer Diversity: A Rainbow of Opportunities* (Heritage Arts, 1992) explore other techniques of recruiting and welcoming many different people as volunteers.

In the last analysis, you cannot expect all volunteers to become friends. But you can expect people to work together to accomplish mutual goals. People of different backgrounds may initially be uncomfortable if they feel unfamiliar with each other. But you will also find that volunteers enjoy getting to know people they would not typically encounter in their daily routine. Start with what they already share in common: having said yes to becoming a volunteer in support of the same organization! The rest will come with cooperation and time.

Not the Last Thought on Diversity

Our purpose in this book is to consider all the issues that have an impact on recruiting volunteers. This chapter has therefore approached the topic of diversity with a narrow focus: how to open the door to attract more varied volunteers. But "diversity" is a much bigger and more important subject that deserves your attention and self-education.

I encourage you to do whatever is necessary to broaden participation within your organization. You may need to work together with your director, human resources department, and other key staff to consider the question of diversity among employees as well as among volunteers. You may need to hold training workshops that enable everyone to build trust relationships and discover each other's talents. Diversity is more than an end unto itself—it is one of the ways to enlist every possible resource in the accomplishment of your organization's mission. And it makes life so much more interesting!

Appealing to Special Target Audiences

All of the principles discussed so far have universal application. But there are some special issues to consider when approaching certain target audiences. This is because every segment of our society has its own set of concerns and trends. So, if you want to recruit volunteers from a particular group, you must understand and adapt to their frame of reference.

Before you use any of the suggestions in this chapter, be sure you have worked through the recommended recruitment steps, particularly brainstorming potential sources of volunteers (Chapter 6). Only if you have decided that one of the target populations discussed in the next few pages is *the right source* for your needs should you look here for some additional tips and pointers in seeking out and asking these target audiences to become volunteers for your organization.

One way to approach any specific population is to ask: how can I address these people's needs while trying to meet my organization's needs? Let's examine a number of prospective volunteer talent pools with this question in mind. In each section I'll outline some of the issues to consider when appealing to this target group and share some practical points on crafting your message appropriately.

Students

Students are a very large category of potential volunteers. Consider the range of students available:

- Graduate students
- College students
- High school students from public, private and parochial schools
- Younger students from the lower grades

In addition, there is variety in how such students might come to you:

- On their own
- Through a formal service-learning program in which the volunteer work is integrated into the classroom curriculum
- Through a club or project (based either at the school or with a youth agency) in which students do the volunteer work as an extra-curricular activity
- Because of a requirement to complete a certain number of hours of "community service" before graduation

As a recruiter, each of these options suggests a different recruitment approach. In some cases your goal will be to communicate to students directly; in other situations you will need to motivate faculty or adult leaders first. The point is to be as specific as possible when doing the exercise of "where can I find students who _____ (have X skill or interest)." To demonstrate, look at the following list and think about how each source will lead you to very different skills, interests, and possible motivations of students (even from the same school):

- A class in home economics
- A class in fourth-year Spanish
- The dining hall
- A student assembly
- The gymnastics team
- The student government
- The school library
- A fraternity

There is nothing new about students as volunteers. But as we have already discussed in the chapter on trends and issues (see page 38), there is currently a big push to develop formal, school-based "community service" or "service-learning" projects. If you have a local school district or university with such a project, get connected.

Apart from the possibility of having to fulfill a *requirement* to do a certain amount of service, students respond very well to volunteer recruitment that emphasizes that volunteering:

- is a way to test skills
- adds a new dimension to a résumé
- is a form of career exploration
- builds a network of contacts for a job search later

Beware the tendency to use youngsters solely for their energy and willingness to do physical labor. There is nothing wrong with walk-a-thons and yard clean-ups, but you are missing some great ideas if you do not give young people the chance to be part of the adult team. Learning comes from being involved in all aspects of a project, so allow young volunteers to help with planning and follow-up as well as implementation.

If you hope to be bringing in many young volunteers, it may be advantageous to form some sort of "youth advisory council" to involve teenagers and other students from the beginning of the process. As with other similarly-suggested task forces with special expertise, such a youth council can help you to design interesting student volunteer assignments, identify the best places to recruit young people, and grapple with any other issues relevant to making the participation of this age group work successfully.

Other Sources of Young People

Keep in mind that there are lots of other places to locate young people other than schools. In fact, for some youngsters, being offered the opportunity to volunteer through the referral of a teacher may be exactly why it does *not* sound appealing!

In addition to seeking individuals, you may very well want to link with youth-serving organizations who can offer you the volunteer effort of *groups* of young people, often with adult leadership already built in. Possible sources include:

- church youth groups
- Girl and Boy Scout troops, Camp Fire, 4-H, etc.
- recreation centers
- playing fields and swimming pools
- summer camp programs
- after-school activities at various community organizations
- music, dance or art classes at private academies
- Sunday schools
- juvenile detention centers
- group homes

These sites may provide young volunteers for one-time group projects or for short-term activities that allow the sponsoring group to get credit for its contributed effort.

Be open to non-traditional sources of help. For three years in a row, the teenage residents of area detention centers and group homes have stuffed the registration packets for the annual state conference of the Virginia Office of Volunteerism.

Families

The term "intergenerational" is usually used too narrowly, referring to seniors working with children. In truth, any project is intergenerational if it recruits more than one age group at a time. For some volunteer programs, families volunteering together, as a unit, may be an excellent source of help.

The key to recruiting families is to design work of interest to both parents and children so that the younger members of the family can be equal participants, not drag-alongs. Families can be recruited by soliciting the parents first or the younger members first. While families can be found "everywhere," you should follow the brainstorming rules for focusing your search to identify the most likely families that might want to volunteer with you. For example:

- If you are in a parks and recreation setting, look for families who go camping together at a nearby campground, or bowl together at the local lanes, or bike together on Saturday mornings in the park.

- Consider which sites bring families together anyway: religious congregations, pediatricians' offices, youth sports events, children's clothing stores.

- If your organization serves children as a client group, be aware that older siblings sometimes feel left out of the picture. They may feel frustrated at not being able to help and amazed at your invitation to contribute their talents as volunteers.

Seniors

Common wisdom has it that senior citizens volunteer a great deal. While there are many older volunteers, the data shows us that a smaller percentage of seniors contribute their time than people in most other age categories. One reason for this is the wide range of age covered by the label "senior." As a recruiter, it is very helpful to distinguish between the three segments of the older population, each of which has different needs to which you can speak as you recruit:

Younger seniors: Ages sixty to seventy or so, who either recently retired or perhaps are still working at a paying job, are in generally good health, have a degree of discretionary income, and are mobile. For them, volunteering is a way to stay connected to previous interests or to make a complete switch in "careers."

Middle seniors: Ages seventy to eighty-five or so, who have settled into the concept of retirement, are less mobile (have perhaps given up their cars), have concerns for safety and not being out at night, and are beginning to show physical signs of aging. Volunteering can be a way to maintain health and give a sense of belonging as they begin to lose family and friends.

Older seniors: Age eighty-five and above, who may be frail but who increasingly are living with greater capacities and for whom volunteering is a way to remain alert and active. But they may not be able to come to you to do the work.

Most seniors are quite capable of explaining their abilities, restrictions, and choices to you. You will find some older volunteers who are pleased to do work to help their peers. But be prepared for the senior who tells you in no uncertain terms that he or she wants to "get away from the old fogeys"! The opportunity to stay connected with younger people may be a primary reason for some older volunteers to sign up.

As the population ages, there are many new places to look for seniors: retirement communities, special college course programs, Elderhostel, pre-retirement counseling workshops, senior centers. Remember RSVP (page 57) and the other Older American volunteer programs of the Corporation for National and Community Service. Large corporations may have ways for you to contact their retirees (see next section). Even nursing homes can be a source of volunteers, if you have work that can be brought in to the residents.

Recruitment materials targeted at seniors should be in easily-legible type, with strong contrast to the background. Always avoid red ink which is hard to read for people with cataracts. Speak to issues of transportation and safety, and try to offer reimbursement for out-of-pocket expenses (fixed incomes can leave little room for volunteer costs).

Corporations

We have already discussed the trend of for-profit businesses encouraging their employees to do volunteer work. How can you access such projects? It depends both on the way a company is organized and for what type of project you are trying to recruit.

Keep in mind that the company may be approached daily by many other community organizations. Be sure there is a clear "link" between your agency and the interests of this particular business. For example, are their customers your clients? Is their product or service connected in some way to your work? Are they located very close to your site? Are any of their employees clients or volunteers of yours?

Much has been written about "work release" programs in which employees are given time off during the day, while on salary, to do community service. In truth, very few companies have such programs. But many permit some "flex time," whereby an employee is allowed to take the youth group camping on Friday afternoon and can make up the time the next week, or can take two hours for lunch to deliver homebound meals and then stay an hour later the same day. The majority of employee volunteer programs, however, encourage employees to do volunteer work on their own time with the company serving as a source of information for what can be done and sometimes as a provider of support resources. An example of the latter is the team of employees who plant new trees on a Saturday morning, using a truck and tools on loan from the company and receiving company logo tee-shirts to keep as a recognition gift. Finally, some companies maintain active communication with their retired employees and try to use community service as a group activity for them.

Often your first contact source will be the company's Public Affairs or Community Relations office. This is the most common "home" of an employee volunteer effort. For obvious reasons, these staffers are interested in demonstrating that the company is a "good neighbor." Another possibility for recruiting employee volunteers is working with whoever is responsible for charitable contributions. This person may be frustrated at dealing with many requests for money and a limited pool of funds. Maybe your request for the help of the company's people rather than the company's money will be welcomed. On the other hand, some corporations have a "Dollars for Doers" program in which a financial contribution is made to the nonprofit agency in which an employee serves as a volunteer—something of a corporate "match" for the employee's gift of time.

If there is no formal community outreach program, see if you can enlist the help of the editor of the company's in-house newsletter. In some cases, you can work with the Marketing Department, if the project has a direct tie-in to a sales effort (this is sometimes called "cause-related marketing"). Yet another access point is the person who organizes company recreational events (group travel, bowling tournaments, etc.). After all, a lot of group volunteering is fun to do and can be "pitched" as a chance to do good while socializing.

While corporations are excellent sources of individual volunteers, they are especially useful as sources of teams or groups of employees needed for one-time or short-term projects. The exchange for the company is that team volunteering increases morale among the employees and gives the business itself greater visibility. This is why teams often show up in company tee-shirts or caps. Group activities also have a better chance of obtaining supportive resources such as tools or equipment, either as a donation or on loan.

One good way to select a company is to start with the employers of current volunteers, letting the employee begin the contact for you.

Small Businesses

For most volunteer efforts, a Fortune 500 company is less viable as a recruitment source than is the small, local company. Small business (which ranges in size from the mom-and-pop corner store to companies employing a hundred people) frequently has a greater vested interest in your community. After all, it is their community, too. All the decision-makers as well as the employees will be local citizens.

As do larger businesses, small businesses want the halo effect of being connected in the public eye with a good cause—in the hope that they will elicit new customers while doing something charitable. As always, my advice is to have a logical reason why you are approaching any business— what do you have in common? Proximity is an excellent conversation starter for a local business. Not only can you point out that their employees might volunteer with you on their lunch hour or on the way home from work, but the company might also give you access to their customers—who also must pass by your facility. Access can mean letting you leave flyers for customers to take, creating a window display about your organization, or any other creative (and mutually-beneficial) type of communication.

You can find small businesses with potential as a volunteer source by doing your "Proximity Chart" (pages 49-52), brainstorming connecting links and using the Yellow Pages, or working through the Chamber of Commerce. There may also be trade associations, neighborhood business associations, and special groups such as associations of women business owners.

Sole Practitioners

Sole practitioners are a special category of small business. The diversity of people in business for themselves is staggering. The list includes accountants, artists, architects, writers, lawyers, and consultants of every type. The common denominator among these professionals is that their time is measured in "billable hours." But they also have enormous discretion in what to do with their time and how to schedule themselves. This means that a sole practitioner can choose to volunteer with you and "make up" the billable hours at another time.

Clearly, these people have specific skills to offer and can be excellent volunteer resources. You can find them in the same way you look for small, local businesses (which they are). Some of the approaches that work well include gaining visibility for their skills, new client development, and possibly some barter of their expertise for something your agency has that they may need: storage space, access to a color copier, a parking space. Remember that people who are in business for themselves are the boss; they do not need to ask permission from anyone if they choose to volunteer.

Professional Firms

There are large and small professional firms (lawyers, accountants, doctors, architects, etc.), all of which have a great deal in common with other businesses. But as a recruiter you need to under-

stand that decisions are reached in a less hierarchical fashion, by vote of all the partners. Professional firms rarely employ a public affairs staff member, instead allowing their professional staff to pursue any interest that leads to "client development." So your job as a recruiter is to show the connection between volunteer work and visibility in the community.

Some firms encourage the use of a certain percentage of "billable hours" in community service—or *pro bono*—activities. If all else fails to get free services, you may be able to negotiate a special reduced fee.

Professional Societies and Trade Associations

It may be easier to tap professional skills by going through a state (or local) professional society. Every profession, occupation, and trade has an association, though some will be more formal than others. In general, such societies hold regular business meetings and annual conferences or conventions, and publish some sort of newsletter or other publications. All have a board of directors and the larger associations have paid staff. There may even be a public service committee seeking community projects.

When you approach a professional society, be very clear on what the exchange of benefits will be. Explain why you need the skills offered by the members and respect the fact that usually they are paid for these services. Show how the society will gain by giving its members the chance to participate with you: visibility, morale, client development opportunities. Use the vocabulary of *"pro bono"* work.

Usually you will approach a professional or trade association to gain access to the special skills of its members. But you can also go "against type" and recruit members for a volunteer project that is a complete change from their daily routine. One of the best examples of this type of volunteering is the "1040K Run" sponsored for a number of years by the Georgia Society of CPAs. It pitted CPAs against staff of the local IRS office! All the money raised went to charity. Think of all the stereotypes about accountants that this type of athletic event counteracted.

Make your first contact with the paid staff person in charge of public relations or with someone on the board of directors. If you have a volunteer now who is a member of this profession, the natural approach would be to ask him or her to start the ball rolling.

Organized Groups of All Sorts

Given the enormous number of civic and social clubs and associations in any community, it is hard to find many common denominators—except that they all rely on volunteer members to do the work and run the organization. Because of this you want to work with organized groups to meet their membership development needs, not to compete with them. If you can identify projects that allow the group to gather its members as a team, or even to recruit new group members in order to participate in your volunteer project, then you have a good chance for success.

Your first task is to nurture the officers of the organized group. They will know the best way to approach their members and can give you access to people individually and at meetings. As with all the other resources we have been discussing, if you have a volunteer now (or paid staff member, for that matter) who is a member of the group, start with her or him.

For more tips on reaching out to organized groups, go back to the section on public speaking in Chapter 7.

Churches and Other Religious Institutions

Every denomination has different ways of organizing its religious and lay activities. Some common features are clergy, religious/moral education of children, adult education, social activities, holiday programs, and some way to demonstrate *social concern*. This is built into the tenets of most of the religions practicing in North America today. Historically, churches, synagogues, mosques, meetings and temples contributed enormously to the charitable and social life of their communities. And this remains true today. Some congregations

understand the use of the word "volunteer," but others will be more responsive to a recruiter who speaks about social concern or "lay ministry."

Religion, as any other element of society, is undergoing changes. On one hand, attendance at traditional services is declining. But on the other hand, people are actively seeking new ways to experience and express their religious beliefs. If you approach church leaders, be alert to their needs for strengthening the congregation. How can you develop a mutually-beneficial working relationship?

Approach a religious body for help with clients who live in that church's parish/neighborhood. Link the project to a religious holiday, suggest a sermon on the importance of charity, or find a way to involve several Sunday school classes (on the premise that this is practice in what has been preached!).

Larger congregations may actually have a Volunteer Coordinator in a staff position, who would obviously be your first contact point. There may be a Social Concerns Committee or other lay leadership group which plans church activities. While the clergyperson may seem the natural contact point, this person is a busy administrator and spiritual leader with many demands on his or her time. It is generally more effective to begin with someone who can concentrate on your request. As with other sources of volunteers, the best idea is to work through an individual church member who already has some sense of affiliation with your organization—a current volunteer or staff member. This person will know the ropes of making the right contacts in this congregation and will be your best spokesperson.

One innovative idea was described by Kathleen Brown in *Voluntary Action Leadership* (1985). Under the name "Share the Heart" project, the Community Congregational Church in Tiburon, California asked community agencies for *one-time* volunteer jobs that church members could do individually or in small groups in four hours or less.[1] Two Sundays were set aside for "Share the Heart"; the minister built his sermon on the value of community involvement. When the service ended, the congregation found several large bulletin boards at the back of the church, covered with index cards explaining the various projects available. Each person selected and committed to a project. This idea provided community agencies with a large pool of talent and energy (albeit in four-hour doses), provided the church with a religiously-connected team activity, and introduced many individuals to the possibilities of volunteering. Could you adapt this idea in some way?

In some localities, you may be able to work through organized coalitions of churches (either of the same denomination or ecumenical). Such groups, often called some variation of "Interfaith Council" or "Urban Ministries," have been formed to address community-wide concerns and may therefore be excellent conduits for your recruitment efforts. On the other hand, some religious bodies may be feeling inundated with requests for help. If these congregations are already hard at work providing food pantries for the homeless, sanctuary to political dissenters, or after-school care to latch-key children, they may truly be overextended. If you reach out to local churches and synagogues, become informed about the causes each considers most vital and offer your volunteer opportunities as a form of partnership in addressing mutual concerns.

The Military

If you live in a community with a military installation, make use of this talent resource. All the branches of the military have formal community service programs designed to connect service people with their temporary neighborhoods. You want to make your first contact through one of the following offices:

Army: Either the Installation Volunteer Coordinator, the Army Community Service office, or the Commander of the Installation.

Navy: Either the Ombudsman office or the Family Service Center.

Air Force: Family Support Center Director

Marines: Family Service Center Director

Coast Guard: Morale, Welfare and Recreation office (though most Coast Guard units are quite small and you can work with anyone in charge).

The first interest of these offices is support of military personnel and much of the volunteering they coordinate is of a self-help nature for families on the base: youth sports programs, substance abuse counseling, marriage counseling. But they are also mandated to work with their local communities and will be able to suggest ways you can recruit both active military personnel and their families as volunteers.

In addition to the formal staff, all military posts have *spouse clubs* that can be contacted directly. There is often an officers' spouse club and one for enlisted personnel. As with all voluntary membership groups, the contact people change as presidents and committee chairs rotate out of office. But many of these clubs seek out community service projects. The same is true of *retired* military personnel associations, many of which maintain a connection with a particular installation.

When you work with the military, keep in mind that transience is part of the job. Volunteers may be called to active duty on very short notice, including transfers to other bases—and this includes your contact person, too. But while in your area, service people welcome new leisure time activities and their spouses may enjoy the diversion from post life.

The National Guard, Army Reserves, and Coast Guard Auxiliary should also be considered as resources for certain types of volunteer needs. They can be asked to help with one-day group projects or to loan such things as tents and outdoor supplies.

Program Participant-Volunteers

There are three types of participant-volunteers:

People who are themselves receiving the services of your organization but are also willing to join the volunteer corps to help others. In this form of involvement, you want to tap the talents of clients/consumers because they bring a perspective or set of skills not otherwise available. Also, this may be a way of building self-esteem or even teaching employable skills. Basically, these participant volunteers blend into your regular volunteer corps. There is not necessarily any reason to distinguish

123

them from any other volunteer, unless their assignment is to be a partner to another client or specifically to be a program advisor. A variation of this idea is to recruit "alumni"—people who have successfully completed their time as a recipient of service (or whose precipitating need has ended) and now are able to be of help to others still in need.

"Members" of your participant pool who are asked to assume leadership roles as an extension of membership. The best way to explain this option is the example of a senior center. Any senior citizen in a given geographic area may be eligible to join the center and participate in all its activities. But in order to get daily work done or to plan special events, you need some members to volunteer time and/or leadership. The key here is that while anyone may take part in the center's activities, you may want to be more selective in who fills volunteer positions. So you may need to do some thoughtful recruiting.

Self-help groups (see page 136 in "Alternatives to Recruitment"). This means clients helping clients in a mutual-aid model.

The trick in recruiting service recipients to also become volunteers is making sure that there is a clear exchange of benefits. What is the rationale for asking a client or participant to contribute time? Is volunteering a way for the client to have input into program service methods or plans? Is it, in fact, preferable to involve volunteers with a personal understanding of the problem in reaching out to others—and does this, in turn, help the participant-volunteer to gain more support as well?

If you are serving a low-income population, it may be important to facilitate volunteer involvement by reimbursing out-of-pocket expenses. Certainly you should be sensitive about assuring comfortable interaction with volunteers of greater means, including such issues as whether participant-volunteers feel they have appropriate clothing. But, as always, never assume that lack of money means lack of concern or capability. On the other hand, lack of education may be a more difficult barrier to effective service. If your client population includes people who are functionally illiterate, you may have to adapt your volunteer job descriptions to require no or less reading and

writing. After that, you may be surprised at the ways non-readers can be reservoirs of amazing talents.

Exercise caution against "typecasting" clients. Someone may initially become involved with your organization at a time of need but can then grow well past that point. This is another great reason for seeking the potential abilities latent in everyone.

Employees as Volunteers

Some organizations take pride in noting that a number of their own employees also contribute personal time as volunteers to the organization. This is certainly a lovely indicator of caring and concern, but I need to caution you.

First, this practice runs the danger of violating the federal Fair Labor Standards Act, which prohibits an employer from expecting employees to work overtime without proper compensation. Even if the employee's volunteer activity is completely voluntary, it is essential to do several things to document compliance with the Act:

- have a clear volunteer job description that is demonstrably different from the employee's ordinary job description;

- make the employee "apply" to become a volunteer;

- assign the employee to volunteer work in a different unit and with different clients than in his or her ordinary work with the organization; and

- keep completely separate records on the employee's time contributed and accomplishments as a volunteer.

If in doubt, talk to your agency's attorney.

Second—and perhaps most important—be absolutely sure that no employee feels coerced in any way to become a volunteer. "Coercion" can sometimes be subliminal. If your organization holds an annual fundraising bazaar and, over the years, it has become "traditional" for all employees to volunteer for a shift of duty, this may be perceived as an unremunerated *expectation* of the job. The same is true if a so-called volunteer activity is felt to be desired by a supervisor in charge of pay increases or promotions.

I am not telling you to ban employees from becoming volunteers, but I recommend that you analyze *why* this is happening and whether, in the long run, this pool of people is giving you the same help you would get from more aggressive recruitment of outside volunteers. After all, how can you expand the talents already available if your paid and unpaid staff are the same people? Burnout is a real possibility, too.

If an employee really wants to contribute volunteer time to your organization, consider making her or him a "loaned" volunteer assigned to a collaborating community partner. See the ideas in "Alternatives to Recruitment" (Chapter 13).

Untapped or Undertapped Resources

If you follow the approach to recruitment suggested in this book, you will brainstorm a wide variety of unexpected places to look for new volunteers. No source is off limits. The truth is that most organizations return repeatedly to the same small circle of sources and never try new avenues. To demonstrate this point, here are four examples of what I consider to be untapped, or at least under-tapped, pools of prospective volunteers:

The trades: Because there is a history of tension between labor unions and volunteers in some settings, volunteer programs tend to assume that blue collar workers are not interested in volunteering. This is a form of mental conversation! If you would not hesitate to ask a time management expert to conduct a workshop for free (even though s/he usually gets paid to do so), why not ask the roofer to fix the roof for free? Remember the principle: if you never ask, you certainly won't get.

There are a number of ways to reach skilled trades people, not all of whom are unionized. Yes, you can collaborate with labor unions, most of whom have social concern committees and already do many charitable things. You can work with trade and vocational schools, perhaps with their alumni groups. You can reach tradespeople through various suppliers and vendors, too.

Some government-funded programs may have to learn the restrictions of the Davis-Bacon Act before asking for *any* volunteer help in construction or renovation. The booklet from the Nonprofit Risk Management Center, "Legal Barriers to Volunteer Service" (1994), gives you some guidelines. But most organizations have the freedom to ask for whatever volunteer help they need.

Teachers: With all the discussion of students as volunteers, we sometimes overlook that faculty members are also candidates. You can recruit teachers (any school grade or university) with their classes, or offer volunteer assignments in after-school hours or in the summers. Teachers need ways to learn new things for themselves and to be valued as contributors to adult causes. It is easy to feel typecast as youth-oriented only. The same holds true for principals and school district administrators.

Corporate middle managers: Just as teachers can be overlooked in all the discussion about students, middle managers are frequently left out of the "employee volunteering" picture. Top management is in demand for board of directors positions and frontline employees are the targets for hands-on volunteer recruitment. Middle managers do not yet have the status to be sought after for boards, but may welcome the chance to demonstrate their community leadership potential. Also, they may want to join in the "team spirit" of group volunteering with their supervisees, but may feel a bit unwelcome if the volunteer activity is done on people's own time. A special invitation in such a case can work wonders.

Night shift workers: People whose work hours differ from the majority are motivated by the same things as any other prospective volunteer. If we expect people who work Monday to Friday, 9:00 a.m. to 5:00 p.m., to become volunteers in their "free" time (evenings and weekends), why not make the same assumption about people who work different shifts? Who better to help serve breakfast at the shelter than someone who is wide awake at 7:00 a.m.? To recruit night shift workers, you have to get the message across *at night*—which is why we rarely think about this potential pool of people. Night shift workers get a "lunch" break just as day workers do. So all the cafeteria displays and other recruitment techniques can be used for this group, as well.

There is nothing mysterious about encouraging night shift workers to volunteer: go to them and ask. This may mean arranging to send someone from your organization to a worksite in the evening to talk with prospective candidates. Target a worksite with a campaign that shows employees you really want their involvement. The "we're in the same neighborhood" approach makes sense to people. So do volunteer job descriptions that make use of the skills these employees demonstrate on their paying jobs (though leave room for them to select a volunteer assignment that offers them a change of pace).

You get the point, I'm sure. Be creative and recruit folks who have rarely been invited in.

[1] Kathleen M. Brown, " 'Share the Heart': An Innovative Way to Involve Church Members in the Community," *Voluntary Action Leadership* (Summer 1985), p. 19.

Membership Development

The similarities between recruiting volunteers to work in an agency and recruiting members to join an association are greater than the differences. For predominantly-volunteer groups there is the additional issue of transforming "members" into active workers—people willing to do necessary projects, hold office, chair committees. In fact, this is one of the distinctions between the *voluntary* act of joining an organization and becoming a *volunteer* on behalf of that organization. Having many names on the membership rolls does not necessarily mean having enough help to achieve goals.

The material in this chapter is relevant to just about any type of all-volunteer group (or organization comprised of many members and just a few paid support staff). Your particular interest(s) may be as diverse as a civic club, professional society, trade association, or co-op board. Note that everything here can be applied to a DOVIA (the generic term for associations of Directors Of Volunteers In Agencies)!

A special category of "all-volunteer" organization is churches (and synagogues, mosques, and meetings). Although a church is also an institution, the way in which congregations work is by voluntary agreement and the contributions (money and time) of their members. In the United States, participation in any religious body is non-mandated. The decision to join is voluntary and accepting an active role in the work of the congregation makes someone a volunteer. So the suggestions in this chapter for the officers of any all-volunteer group are fully applicable to clergy and lay leaders as well.

Finally, you may be a director of volunteers with an agency that has an all-volunteer support group such as an auxiliary, friends group, or special events fundraising body. Although the officers of these associations are the ones with primary responsibility for membership development, you may be the liaison staff member or act as a consultant to them. This chapter may be of help.

Getting People to Join

Membership development is a process that follows the same sequence of steps as any other form of volunteer recruitment.

Step 1: *Define your membership goals.*

—Do you need sheer numbers (for political clout or the increase in dues revenue) or do you want to find members who will contribute their time and talents in an active way?

—Are there any special target audiences from whom you most want to draw new members?

—How many members do you want?

—Does it matter whether your members are active or not?

Step 2: *Define what "membership" means in your organization.*

—What are the benefits and the responsibilities of members?

—What are the qualifications for becoming a member?

—What are the costs?

—Why would someone want to join?

—What should a new member expect from you in terms of meetings, types of communication, opportunities to meet others, etc.?

—How long do you expect/hope that people will remain members?

Step 3: *Brainstorm where in your community you might locate people who suit your desired profile of a good member.*

Step 4: *Select a technique to match the sources identified.*

Step 5: *Do it.*

Sound familiar?

All the principles discussed in this book apply to membership development. Such as:

- Do not assume people know about your organization or that you are looking for new members.

- Be alert to the public image of your organization and whether you might have to counteract some historic misconceptions.

- Articulate the benefits of membership (using the reasons why people may want to join up).

- Diagnose why some people may be reluctant to join and see if you can assuage their concerns (or if you need to remove some gravy stains!).

- To get results, you really need to *ask* people to join.

- The clearer you can be about what joining means (like the agency job description), the more success you will have—and the more prospective applicants can self screen themselves.

- Apply the McDonald's Quotient and repeat your message regularly.

Asking yourself the questions about image in Chapter 4 is a good idea, too. An all-volunteer organization also does not operate in a vacuum.

Your Current Membership

Examine who is joining your organization now. Can you see similarities among the members? Specifically list the characteristics of your members. Use whatever demographic data interests you: gender, age, race, where people live, professions, etc. Are you diverse (and is this something that matters to you)?

Now discuss *why* the membership has come to look this way. Has membership development been accidental or intended? Who is in charge of recruiting new members, what recruitment activities have occurred in the past few years, and what has been the result? In most situations, the key discovery is that no one has been masterminding membership development. No one is out there systematically inviting people to join. If this is what you conclude for your group, everything we have been saying in the previous chapters applies to you now.

Using your current members to attract new ones makes a lot of sense, of course. But just as we have noted with agency volunteers, this process might not just happen naturally. Set certain times for consciously encouraging members to invite guests to a meeting or event. Perhaps designate one month a year for a big recruitment push—and use friendly competition to add spice to the process, giving prizes to successful recruiters.

Give members *tools* with which to spread the word. Make sure everyone has extra membership brochures. Or you might consider printing a special piece for members to give their friends that begins with something like: "You may have wondered about my membership in XXX . . . let me tell you more. . . ." Some quick training in *how* to recruit might be helpful, too.

Sometimes current members can identify friends or contacts who are likely prospects for recruitment, but are hesitant to approach these people personally. Their reluctance stems from not wanting to pressure friends. So one idea is to buddy up two or more members and have them each contact the *other person's* list of names. The recruiter can explain the source of the referral, but the prospective member has the option of turning down the offer to join without feeling obligated or worrying about insulting the referring friend (how can you say nicely, "I'm not interested in the group you care so much about"?).

The one caution I can give is the same as for any one-to-one recruitment: people will recruit people who are like themselves. So if you are happy with the diversity of your membership, then by all means plan your membership development efforts around current member outreach. But if you want to expand your circle to include different ages, races, or parts of the community, you will need a different approach. You will need to solicit members from among people none of you already knows.

If you have been trying to recruit new members without much success, or trying to diversify the membership without success, diagnose why there might be resistance to joining, as we discussed in Chapter 3. However, also spend time thinking about how open current members are to newcomers. Is there genuine desire to bring in new people, especially if they are different in some way from the average member now?

Initiating Real Change

The question of merging veteran members and newcomers (especially if the new people are different in some way from the traditional norm for your group) deserves some additional attention. Many all-volunteer efforts have a social purpose that is as important as their civic contributions. This is why members tend to become homogeneous over time: people make friends with people who are like themselves. While some of this gravitation to similarity may be based on prejudice and discrimination, more often it is rooted in comfortable inertia. It is simply easier to look for members in one's own circle than to do outreach to strangers. Yet the only way to transform strangers into new friends is to do outreach.

For some readers, the question of recruiting new and possibly diverse members is one of survival. The sad fact is that some groups are dying, either through atrophy or actual aging of their members. How do you salvage an organization that has been fading for a long time?

The truth is that resuscitation is very hard. Too often a group waits too long to freshen up its membership rolls. It is a hard sell to recruit new members into an organization that has clearly seen better days or to expect a handful of young people (or men or any other group) to feel comfortable surrounded by a majority of members much older than themselves (or all women or whatever).

This subject probably warrants a book by itself. The reason I raise it here is that a recruiter must be realistic. If the situation your group faces is this serious, maybe a "membership campaign" is the wrong strategy. Perhaps you would be better off sponsoring a *project* for which you recruit non-member volunteer workers. The people you recruit can be more diverse and your goal is for the project, initially, to be an end unto itself. Let these volunteers have a good time and a successful experience. Current organization members might not even participate, except perhaps in support roles.

Afterward, call a post-project evaluation meeting and discuss how this project fits into your overall organizational goals. Be honest about the status of your membership today. Engage project participants in considering whether they might want to join the "parent" organization together . . . or whether they want to start an affiliate group.

The point is to generate interest for your *cause,* letting the question of "joining" as a member come naturally after some exposure to you. To get many more creative ideas about encouraging wider participation from new and old members, read *When Everyone's a Volunteer* by Ivan Scheier (Energize, 1992).

Getting Members to Work

For some organizations, the problem is not recruiting new members. The real concern is that too many current members are inactive, do not participate in meetings or projects, and resist committing to leadership roles.

Few things are more frustrating than watching (or being one of) a small group of members burning themselves out doing all the work of an organization, growing increasingly upset at the ungrateful, apathetic majority. The key to organizational health is member participation. How can you mobilize members from passivity into action?

The truth is that many people join a group without ever *intending* to be active or to do any work—and they have absolutely no idea that you

129

expect this of members anyway. Joining involves many factors. Sometimes people want to show support for a cause and are happy to affiliate themselves with you. They may consider their dues as a form of contribution, letting you use the money well. In other cases, people join in order to receive your publications; they feel connected largely by keeping themselves informed through your newsletters or journals. If you have other, tangible benefits of membership, these may be the major motivators. But if someone joins up solely for the discounts, the insurance, or the group travel, do not be surprised if you never see this member at a planning meeting! For some organizations, the way to get a stronger core of active volunteers may be to *reduce* the external benefits and thus weed the rolls of nonproductive members.

It may be necessary for your board of directors to reassess the goals of membership development. For some groups, the size of membership on paper is indeed more important than the number of people who come to meetings or help at events. Or, if the group's purpose is public education or some form of advocacy, it may be wonderful to have hundreds of readers of the monthly newsletter, regardless of whether anyone ever meets a member in person. For a professional society, signing up a majority of the practitioners in any one region may be the first goal, with ideas for what to do with them coming later. In all these cases, the emphasis should be on getting new and more members (and then retaining them on the rolls each year).

But the majority of associations, societies and clubs hope for healthy numbers of members *and* active participation.

Before anything else, take a look at the way you recruit members to join in the first place. Read over your association brochure or your application form. Consider the oral presentations you make. Do you spend all of your time telling prospective members what the organization will do *for them?* When, if ever, do you mention what you hope members will do *for the organization?* So my first suggestion is to define what you expect from a member in return for the benefits received:

Attendance at Meetings: Do you want attendance at meetings? Why? This is not self-evident. If your meetings are basically social events, or lis-

tening to committee reports and a guest speaker, recognize that this type of evening will only appeal to a percentage of your members. Others may feel that this type of meeting wastes their time every month. On the other hand, if your meetings are the times when you engage members in discussing future projects, reach collective decisions, assign tasks, and perhaps conduct some training, then attendance may be quite important for everyone. If the latter is your situation, consider *stating a requirement* for meeting attendance in the annual membership application form (" . . . must attend at least half of the monthly meetings each year. . . .").

Service Hours: Consider establishing a requirement for the minimum number of hours of service requested from an active member in any given year. Try something like "a minimum of eight hours participating in a work project." Eight hours can be accomplished in one day, if necessary, and therefore allows a member to "work off" the requirement by helping at a special event, completing a mass mailing, or some other "quick and dirty" assignment.

If you decide to set up a service requirement, it is essential that you also develop an accurate record-keeping system to monitor it. Nothing undercuts a requirement faster than non-enforcement—or mistakes. Once you have shown that people can work their eight hours and be properly "credited," while others receive a reminder that their required contribution of time is still pending, you have created a climate of expectation of service.

A service requirement, even one as minor as eight hours, has several purposes. First, it demonstrates that the organization wants the personal involvement of its members (remember that this is not true of every association). Second, by coming out for one long or several short shifts of duty, the member meets other members and has the potential of actually enjoying the participation! This can therefore be a testing ground for more extensive involvement (much like the suggestion of finding ways for prospective agency volunteers to get their feet wet in a short-term assignment before committing to an ongoing one). And third, the contact lets group leaders see the member in action—sort of an audition to observe potential skills or leadership ability.

Committee Work: Some organizations want every member to serve on a committee, though this is mired in tradition that deserves re-evaluation. Often the reason you have trouble recruiting members to join a committee is that they dislike committees! Face it. Committees have a bad reputation as places to go to eat up time by sitting around talking endlessly. Does your organization have many standing committees with little to do? Whenever work has to be done, regardless of how extensive or minimal, does someone say: "let's form a committee"—almost as a kneejerk response? Stop! Carefully consider whether you *need* each committee now in place. Is there truly enough work to assign six to ten people to a year-round planning group? Or could you accomplish the same amount of activity by assigning only one, two or three people to handle it solo or as a small team?

Job Design Issues

Just as with other types of organizations, all-volunteer groups need to be creative in designing the work asked of their members. How long has it been since anyone questioned the purpose of some of your committees, the job descriptions of key positions, or how needed tasks are distributed?

All-volunteer organizations (and churches/synagogues are especially guilty of this) tend to stick with "tradition." What has worked for years becomes fixed in stone, even if there is some evident erosion! Over time, job descriptions lapse but because "everyone knows" what everyone else is doing, leaders are surprised to discover that newcomers feel left out of the insider clique.

Unfortunately, the same is true for who fills certain positions. Members are allowed—even expected—to keep the same job year after year. Terms of office are never discussed. This lack of rotation has serious consequences. First, people burnout and lose enthusiasm for the work. They become "typecast" into their roles and may not know how to graciously extricate themselves. (In some cases, the roles become hereditary, passing from generation to generation!) Second, newcomers have no way in—they quickly learn that all prime roles are taken and may never become available.

I heartily endorse the practice of *requiring* rotation in *all* positions. The number of years someone might work before having to rotate off can vary depending on the demands of the work, but both the volunteer and the organization benefit from a regular freshening up of workers. Rotation can be temporary, as in: "may not hold the position for more than two consecutive terms but may return to the position after at least one term off."

To a recruiter, this may seem like making more work for yourself. If people must rotate, you will have to find new volunteers all the time. In reality, a rotation policy opens the door to new members who bring new enthusiasm. Also, leaders rotating out of a position may be willing to try something completely different for a while.

Another element of job design is how much work is really involved. If your organization is used to relying on homemakers or on businesspeople who order their secretaries to do their backup work, you may have developed job descriptions that are too heavy for today's members. Can existing assignments be broken into smaller chunks of work? Can two members job share one position? Can one member volunteer as a support person for another member, such as being the typist/word processor for a committee chair?

You may also have to be creative in giving members ways they can help with a project even if their schedules seem to conflict. For example, can a volunteer help from home? How about one member providing babysitting for other members who have to set up the bazaar all day Friday?

Just as with agencies, develop ways a new member can test the water before accepting a major responsibility. It is unrealistic to ask someone to join you one month and then run for Vice President the next month. Can newcomers buddy up with experienced members in a sort of apprenticeship (which also gives the current volunteer an "intern" helper)?

How Are Projects Determined?

Who participates in deciding which projects will be selected for the coming year? Think about how decisions are made in your group. Is it an open, public process? Or does the board, for example, determine what will happen this year and then expect members to fall into line and do the work? If you do not find ways to get members to participate in selecting what will be done and how, don't be surprised later if they are unwilling to provide the labor.

Just as in agencies, all-volunteer associations sometimes seek *help* without wanting *input*. It is not easy to get people to come out to planning meetings, but you can at least make a genuine attempt. Then you can test the common wisdom that volunteers work harder for things if they feel a sense of "ownership."

Who Gets Asked

Whenever you see a group of officers sitting around a table considering how to find help on a project, invariably someone asks: "Whom do we know who can do this?" This is *always* a poor question. Why? Because the answer is limited to whom you know! In any association of more than fifty members, it is unlikely that even the officers really know *everyone*.

A much better question is: "whom *don't* we know that we might discover to do this?" And since you are talking about recruiting the involvement of someone who is already a member, this question is even more important.

How can you get to know your members? Once again, analyze your membership and renewal materials. Along with name, address, and telephone number, what else do you ask from new or returning members? For some organizations, it may be appropriate to create a full-fledged application form, asking many of the same questions that an agency volunteer program might want to know about the member's education, skills, or work history. For others, even adding one or two key questions might be extremely useful without turning people off. For example, wouldn't it be helpful to know the present occupation of your members? Or maybe the two things they feel they are most skilled at doing? Or maybe whether they are more accessible during a weekday or on weekends?

If you decide to add profile questions to your membership form, do so only if you develop a plan for *using* the data! I know of many organizations with a wealth of information buried deep in a file cabinet, allowed to grow obsolete with age.

Do not waste the space on the membership form asking essentially useless questions such as: "What committee might you want to join?" As we have already discussed, most new applicants and many veterans have no idea what options are available to them—or can't judge by the name of a committee whether or not it might interest them. Also, since your ability to act on their preference is limited by vacancies on the committees, why set up a scenario for possible disappointment?

It may be a good idea for your group to form a "volunteer development task force" to take the leadership in assuring member involvement. One of the first jobs of the task force would be to "inventory" the membership and begin a recordkeeping system (computers are a great tool these days). The goal is eventually to have a continuously-updated data file of which members are currently assigned to work, which are currently inactive, and which have never been involved. If the data bank also includes information about members' education, talents, interests, and time availability, just think of how useful this can be!

Go through all the names on the rolls and first separate all members currently active in some visible way. Ask these members to complete a "member profile" form asking about their skills and interests—and also asking them to tell the task force their *past roles* with the organization (you want to create a good history at the same time that you want to assess who has been well-utilized, over-utilized, or under-utilized).

For those members not immediately identifiable as assigned to work now, be careful! The task force may not be aware that Lucy is on the Budget Committee or that Rashid is working closely with the Vice President on a special project. You certainly don't want to imply that their work is being done invisibly (though it is!). So you want to begin by asking *every* member to report what s/he is doing now or has done in the past. And then you want them to complete the "member profile."

Whenever possible, if this is a local organization, try to link the member profile with a personal interview. This may sound like an overwhelming suggestion, but it shouldn't be. In the beginning you need to recapture lost information about current members, but later the interviewing will be done mainly with new members (though re-contacting people after three years or so may be a great idea). Interviews can be done by telephone if necessary, but the point is to foster direct, personal contact between leaders of the group and members.

I have frequently suggested that every member of a board or member of a volunteer development task force be given a manageable "quota" of member interview calls to make each month—say, five calls each month. Leaders may express reluctance at making what they perceive as "cold calls" to unknown members. But after all, these are people who have already joined your organization and therefore must share at least some interests. Start the conversations by admitting that you don't know them very well and would like to get better acquainted. Have they considered volunteering for a project?

Even if these members say no, you have gained something as an organization by making active members interact with inactive ones. The important point is that some may say yes (now feeling truly *asked)*, and then you have succeeded in broadening participation.

Nominating Committees

Most organizations use a "Nominating Committee" to develop a ballot of candidates for office or to recommend prospective board members. Usually such a committee is mandated by the bylaws. Unfortunately, Nominating Committees too often convene themselves at the last minute, scramble around for names of people to select, and breathe a sigh of relief when the ballot is in the mail.

In line with the "whom you ask" thoughts in the previous section, a more effective idea is to make the work of the Nominating Committee a year-round, proactive function. One of the earliest articles on the continuous role of the nominating process was written by Phyllis Acker in *The Journal of Volunteer Administration* (Winter 1983-84).

A good first step is to change the committee's name to something like Leadership Development Committee. Among the tasks that could be handled within a broader capacity are:

- Keeping job descriptions updated for all

board and officer positions, committee chair positions, and project roles.

- Being responsible for the gathering and tracking of member profile data and each person's service history.
- Monitoring recognition needed and received (which often is an indicator of when a member is ready to be asked to assume a new position).
- Defining volunteer "career ladders" in which members who wish can advance in degree of responsibility.
- Assuring training of new officers.

In this way, the annual selection of a ballot is part of an ongoing process and should be much easier to do. Committee members will be more informed about who good candidates might be. Also, by being aware of current member involvement, the committee will know about vacancies and about possible lack of diversity.

How You Ask

As I have indicated before, there is a big difference between publicizing an opportunity to volunteer and actually recruiting a candidate to apply for it. So by all means use your newsletter or other publications, or make announcements at meetings, but don't stop there. Remember that if I read about your need for help in the newsletter I know that 500 other people are reading the same article—so you probably "don't mean me." But if you have a personal conversation with me about this task, I definitely understand that I am wanted.

Be cautious of how you ask for help during meetings, especially during full membership sessions. Never say from the podium: "Who wants to do this?" You set up two immediate problems. First, peer pressure tends to work against someone raising his or her hand. (You know the feeling: first there is a pause, then everyone looks around, and the longer no hands are raised, the harder it is for people to "go out on a limb.") Second, it invariably happens that the people who *do* raise their hands are the members you most hoped had stayed home that night!

A better approach is: "We're recruiting for X

position right now. If you want to be considered as an applicant, please see me at the back of the room as soon as we break and I'll give you more details." Then, as the break starts, make yourself visible at the back of the room. The point is to give yourself the flexibility of gathering names and then being able to select the best volunteer.

For a larger organization, it might be a good idea to create an "application form" for leadership positions or even for committee selection. This makes members consider their involvement more consciously and gives you a paper trail to track whether offers of help are indeed being utilized.

What Stops Members from Accepting Leadership Roles

You can make a list of the reasons why some members love to take leadership roles and why others do not—just like we did for any other type of volunteering.

On the plus side are reasons such as:

- great experience
- a way to be in control
- commitment to the cause
- feel it's their turn to serve
- have a martyr complex
- love the adrenaline flow
- gain community status

You can keep the list going. But on the negative side are such factors as:

- afraid they'll become unpopular with their friends
- won't know how to extricate themselves once in
- have watched others before them become burned out
- know exactly how much time it takes and are afraid
- feel their families won't be supportive
- worry that they'll be left holding the bag when others don't do their jobs

These are legitimate fears and may even be an ac-

curate assessment of what your organization does to its leaders. In *When Everyone's a Volunteer,* Ivan Scheier deals at length with the important subject of leader fatigue. The goal for a recruiter or nominating committee member is to make sure the benefits and fun outweigh the problems of accepting a leadership position in your organization.

And What Do We Do with Past Leaders?

It is certainly important to be concerned about welcoming new members and motivating people to move up in the ranks to become organization leaders. But you might also want to take a second look at how your group treats outgoing or past leaders. What happens to the past president and other retiring officers? Do some of them drop off into oblivion, even lapsing their membership after a time? Is there a way to channel these leaders' commitment and vital knowledge into further work on behalf of the organization?

This is a balancing act, of course. You want to provide recognition for past contributions plus hold on to the talents these people possess. *But,* you also want to move such outgoing officers into *new* involvement, not maintain their power and influence to the detriment of the next set of officers. The best advice is to plan for and structure "emeritus" rank participation.

Some organizations have a past-presidents council, which is a fine idea—providing that this council has *tasks to perform.* Other retiring officers might be utilized as trainers or as the nucleus of a new member welcoming committee. Experienced leaders can also be tapped as individual mentors or advisors.

In general, it is a good rule never to assume what an outgoing leader wishes to do. Some might truly welcome a break. Let them have it! Others might have a post-partum depression of sorts and be seeking the right way to continue their contribution of energy. Some may even enjoy starting at the bottom of the leadership ladder again, doing communal work like "any other" member. But if you can offer the *option* of, say, becoming the new member orientation coordinator, you are demonstrating respect and appreciation for their past efforts.

14

Alternatives to Recruitment

After having read an entire book on how to recruit volunteers, it may seem strange to discover a closing chapter on "alternatives to recruitment." But this is consistent with the perspective I presented at the beginning on the role of the leader of volunteers. Remember? Your mandate is to identify needs and then to mobilize noncash community resources to meet those needs. Your goal is *not* necessarily to "sign up" a hundred people as volunteers. The only true measurement of your success is whether or not necessary work gets done.

What are some of the alternatives to recruiting volunteers to do a job directly?

Identify Other Service Providers

Before initiating any new volunteer assignment area, it makes sense to do some community research first. Is anyone already doing the service you need for your clients? What is stopping your agency from making referrals or why won't the other organization accept referrals? It may be the best use of time and effort to establish a good working relationship with an existing community organization rather than developing a competing service.

Perhaps you will need to be creative to make the connection work. For example, if the reason referrals have been limited is that clients lack transportation to get to the other agency, maybe you can arrange for the community organization to send someone on site every other week (bringing the mountain to Mohammed). Or maybe you need to recruit some volunteer drivers to transport clients to the available service (quite a different job description than your original expectation).

Another idea is to form a partnership with the other agency to tap their expertise. If you recruit one to three volunteers willing to help your clients with this service, would the community agency agree to *train* them? We used this plan twenty years ago in my Family Court program in order to provide tutors to teenagers on probation. The local literacy center did not have funding to accept non-adult students, but did have a grant to train reading tutors. So we sent all "our" volunteers to the literacy center to learn how to teach (and the center was able to add those trainees to their statistics on services provided), but then we assigned the volunteers to probationers and provided the ongoing support.

In any such plan, you may have to work out issues such as liability, evaluation and communication systems. Don't let the issue of who gets "credit" for these volunteers stop a potentially great idea. If necessary, give the volunteers the option of a double identity. If they get invited to two recognition banquets in April, is that so bad?

Yet another idea is a staff "exchange." If the community agency agrees to send someone from its staff—employee or volunteer—to provide the service your consumers need, is there some way you can return the favor? Does that agency need the expertise of one of your paid or volunteer staff members in return?

Collaboration

This raises broader concepts of collaboration. Some client needs go well beyond your organization's interests. Instead of struggling alone with recruiting and training a specialized corps of volunteers, perhaps you can share the work—and have an even greater impact.

Consider who might be collaborative partners. As with volunteer recruitment, success depends a lot on choosing the right participants. These can be other community organizations, local businesses, professional societies, schools—almost anyone. Please note that you are not necessarily looking for another organization *similar* to yours. In fact, it is often easier (and less competitive) to collaborate with groups that share a particular interest but clearly have different sets of main goals. For example, if you coordinate a child abuse prevention project, seek out agencies, businesses and community groups which give attention to children but not necessarily about abuse. Or, find other abuse-centered programs even if their focus is not children.

Once you have found collaborative partners, you can share the work of starting a new service. If everyone recruits together, you will spread the word more expansively and quickly. Training can also be done cooperatively, rather than having everyone duplicate independent workshops.

One type of collaboration is another form of piggybacking. Can you use a service already provided in the community to help your clients, too? For example, in some areas of the country, postal carriers have been recruited to monitor elderly residents along their routes. Whenever the mail carrier sees unread mail piling up, s/he knocks on the door and has a brief "friendly visit," or lets a social service agency in town know about the possible problem. Along a similar vein, could a delivery service of any kind be asked to help deliver meals to homebound clients, especially those off the regular routes driven by volunteers now?

A number of years ago the several state institutions all located in Morganton, North Carolina developed an innovative plan to help one another. They recruited employees (who, of course, were also local residents) who wanted to participate (remember the Fair Labor Standards Act) to join volunteer teams. On a regular schedule, these teams rotated among the various institutions, so that one group of employees were volunteers at another team's job site (never at their own site). Given the rural nature of the community, this was a clever way to share the talent pool.

Barter

Barter is a more obvious form of the "exchanges" we have been discussing to encourage volunteers to sign up. Barter is a particularly good way to get the support of small businesses or sole practitioners and it can also be the basis of a collaboration with another agency or with a community group.

First you have to identify what you have that you are willing to *give away* or *share* in exchange for the resource you hope to get. Then, as in regular volunteer recruitment, you identify who might have the skill or item you need and might be interested in what you have to offer. In a strict barter arrangement, the exchange partner may not consider him/herself a "volunteer" (and neither might you). But this does not matter if you accomplish your goal of tapping a needed resource.

What are some examples of barter? See the box on the top of the next page. The list is endless. Some naysayers may warn you that the Internal Revenue Service is watching barter transactions carefully or that a nonprofit has to be careful about mutual benefit arrangements with a business. Some caution is justified and you should research the law. But first find a barter partner with something important to offer your organization—and then work within the law to make the exchange possible.

Client Self-Help

All too often we fall into the trap of seeing the recipients of our services too narrowly, as "in need" only. In truth, the resources to assist clients often are right there, waiting to be tapped. Ironically, if we can facilitate true self-help among clients, we may be providing the best service possible: building self-esteem and "teaching people to fish."

You Need . . .	They Get . . .
Specialized training for volunteers or paid staff in their area of expertise.	Specialized training from you in your area of expertise.
Items to brighten up your walls and hallways.	A venue for displaying their artwork, perhaps even for potential sale.
Access to audiovisual equipment monthly.	Storage space for excess inventory.
Your newsletter designed and printed.	A monthly mailing to be collated.
Use of an office to teach clients how to apply for jobs.	Space for holding larger group meetings.
Seats to be moved/arranged before a concert.	Group tickets to see the concert.

The volunteer office can convene the service-delivery staff to discuss potential areas of client self-help. What can clients do for themselves and what help might they need to get to this point of self-sufficiency? To this end, instead of recruiting volunteers to do something *for* clients, you might be recruiting volunteers to:

- Be buddies or mentors *with* clients.
- Be teachers or role models to *enable* clients to gain new skills.
- Be leaders to *work with* clients in small groups, facilitating their mutual exchange of help.

This whole concept is related to the "spheres of influence" issue discussed earlier. Are there immediate family members or close friends of clients who would welcome the chance to help clients help themselves? What about "alumni" clients who have recently been through your program and can relate to current clients—all the while reinforcing their own progress?

The best advice if you are intrigued by this idea is to convene some clients and talk with them about it. Begin right away to make this *their* project.

Promote Current Volunteers

I have already mentioned that the reasons volunteers stay with an organization may be quite different than the motivations that caused them to join in the first place. Also, as people's lives change, so do their needs and interests. As with paid jobs, people want to "grow" in their volunteer assignments.

Before recruiting new people for vacant volunteer positions, ask current volunteers if they want to be considered for "transfer" or "promotion." Not everyone will want such a change, but it certainly is nice recognition to be *asked*. Also, by asking current volunteers you are publicizing open positions, the first step in enlisting their help to recruit for you. You may find that some volunteers welcome a new challenge—and ultimately stay with you longer by changing jobs than if they had stagnated in a volunteer role that was becoming boring.

If current volunteers want to stay in their present assignment, you can still offer a "leave of absence" to go on "temporary assignment" to help launch a new project, fill a position in the interim while you are recruiting the right volunteer, or contribute a special skill not already being utilized. This can be seen as a perk of the job—a nice change of pace for a short time. By the way, a few people might even be willing to double up assignments temporarily. They can do their regular volunteer work and give some extra hours to accomplish the new task as well. It should be their choice.

Evaluate and Re-design Volunteer Roles

A correlation of the above idea is the need to conduct periodic mutual *evaluations* of current volunteer assignment descriptions. Before you add any new assignments or people, make absolutely certain that everyone is contributing their time in important ways.

When was the last time you evaluated ongoing volunteer assignments? Have some of them become so traditional as to be sacrosanct? Do you suspect that volunteers themselves have developed a vested interest in the assignment itself and have lost track of the overarching goal of doing the most needed tasks?

Here are three real-life examples of "make work" assignments that could (and probably should) be eliminated because ultimately they *waste* volunteer effort. These will strike you as extreme, but think about their implications:

> —*The senior center that tells its printer not to use the automatic folding machine on its order of 5,000 invitations (a cost of no more than $40) because: "doing the folding will give today's volunteers something to do."*

> —*The political campaign manager who has one group of volunteers stuffing envelopes in the front room while another group un-stuffs them in the back room because: "keeping people busy makes them feel af-filiated with the candidate."*

> —*The hospital volunteer director who has a closetful of undistributed baby booties de-spite a decline in maternity care because: "the volunteers have been knitting these for thirty years and love to do it."*

It is hard to believe that there were absolutely no other tasks these volunteers could have done to contribute in a more meaningful way. Very few agencies would purposely waste donated money. Yet contributed time is wasted whenever volunteers are diverted with ancillary tasks while there is vital work to do. And you compound this waste if you go out to recruit *new* volunteers while under-utilizing the ones you have.

Invite current volunteers to help assess how they are utilized now. Be prepared to act on their recommendations, including the possibility of eliminating some roles. You may conclude that the *roles* are still appropriate, but you have the wrong volunteers in them. Promote or transfer the experienced people you have into other assignments and then place newcomers into the vacated task areas.

Cap the Program

Opening the door to new volunteers makes sense only when there is available work for recruits to do. Therefore, one "alternative" to recruitment is to reassess whether you should be doing it at all!

If you are not ready for volunteers . . . don't start to recruit.

If you have too many volunteers to allow them to contribute effectively . . . stop recruiting.

The best thing you can do for your organization and for the people who want to become volunteers is to lay the groundwork for success. Become the in-house advocate for effective involvement of volunteers in your organization. When everything is in place to welcome volunteers, you will be ready to recruit. In time, the reputation you build as a great place to volunteer will ease all your recruitment efforts.

Conclusion

It is my style to wait until a manuscript has been through all its re-writes and is just about ready to go to the printer before trying to write the book's "conclusion." As I review the preceding pages, I am struck by several observations. First, I have literally crammed this book with every suggestion and recommendation on the subject of recruitment I have developed over my twenty-plus years in the volunteer management field. It feels wonderful to have all this out of my head and onto your desk!

Second, there are certain themes that I repeat (and repeat) throughout the book. Each of these bears reiteration because it is central to the logic and vision I bring to the process of recruitment. So, once again:

- You have to be ready to put volunteers to work productively before you can do any recruiting. Don't get "pushed" into recruiting before you have completed the preparation necessary.

- The more creative your organization can become in designing vital work for volunteers to do, the greater your potential to attract all sorts of people to volunteer.

- Find the balance between the needs and dreams of your organization and the motivations and dreams of the people who might want to volunteer with you.

- Success in recruitment is measured only in finding the best people for the positions available—or in finding the right noncash resources to fill a need.

- Focus, focus, focus!

- Keep an eye out for gravy stains.

- Recruiting is connected to, but different from, advertising, public relations, and publicity. Your organization's public image can help or hinder your ability to recruit volunteers.

- Even when you are not consciously recruiting, you're always recruiting! So think about the recruiting consequences/ramifications of everything that you do.

- You are too busy to do any task with only one purpose.

- If someone has expended a lot of time and trouble to plan an event that is relevant to the people you hope to recruit, piggyback on it.

- You don't have to recruit alone. Ask for help inside and outside your organization. (One wonderful thing about our field is that volunteer program managers are really nice to one another. Venture out to a professional meeting and discover that we usually share more than we compete.)

- Never assume potential volunteers know that you need or want them to become involved.

- Make sure you *believe* in what you are asking others to do—believe in the mission of your organization and in the value of volunteering. (Have I said "sincerity wins out over technique" often enough???)

- Don't be afraid to take chances or to break new ground in the way you recruit. Be bold, creative, inventive. It may take a bit of effort to approach a totally new recruitment source or test a nontraditional technique (looking for evening volunteers at the all-night laundromat by giving away detergent with a message wrapped around it)—and it could bomb or it could be great. You'll never know until you try.

- It is always flattering to ask someone to volunteer.

- You can make a friend for your organization even if he or she turns down your invitation to volunteer.

- It takes time for a recruitment message to flourish (growing from all those seeds you'll be sowing!), so don't get discouraged if you hit a dry spell of applicants.

- Diversity means different things to different groups, but to achieve it you may have to become more flexible and adaptable.

- Go out into your community. Read the local newspaper, attend public events, get connected. Be ready to give and share, as well as to ask and get.

- Remember and apply the McDonald's Quotient.

- Have fun while you recruit. If it's O.K. for volunteers to find pleasure in their service, it's O.K. for you, too. Use humor when ap-

propriate. Project the image that volunteering is lively and enjoyable, as well as meaningful.

- In order to recruit new volunteers, you have to *ask people to volunteer* or to join your group.

When people speak about volunteer management, they often say "recruitment and retention" in the same breath. These are clearly related issues, though "retention" is an *outcome*—the *result* of doing things right once a volunteer has joined your organization. While some volunteers want only a short-term involvement, your goal should be to keep every volunteer for at least as long as s/he committed when s/he first signed up. Otherwise, as we have said, the revolving door will only make your recruitment challenge harder.

This book is not the only one you need to develop the best possible volunteer effort. Keep reading and increasing your professional understanding of the full range of important program management subjects: interviewing, screening, training, supervision, evaluation, recognition, recordkeeping, employee/volunteer relations, the role of top administration, and all the other aspects of working successfully with volunteers. The references in this book are only one shelf in your potential library (and compare volunteer management literature to what is being written for employee management, too).

So, the book is finished. I sincerely hope that you have found some useful and perhaps new ideas in these pages. More than anything else, I hope that I have sparked your creativity and given you confidence and encouragement. If nothing else, if someone asks you what McDonald's, gravy, piggybacking, and sowing seeds have to do with volunteer recruitment—you can tell them!

APPENDIX:

OUTREACH IN CYBERSPACE

New to the Third Edition

Internet technology is so new that, in the first edition of this book in 1994, I could only predict briefly that it was an evolving volunteer recruitment technique that would probably become more important over time. Two years later I added an Appendix entitled "The Potential of Cyberspace," in which I said: "This Appendix outlines various electronic recruitment options available today, with the caveat that things are changing so fast that no one can anticipate what the situation will look like in the future—or even next year!" Wow, was I right! Both the capacity and the complexity of this global communication tool multiply continuously, and Internet knowledge becomes obsolete all too quickly. The key point for volunteer recruiters is that cyberspace is irrevocably in our lives and we are all learning together how to get our messages electronically to the most targeted audience.

You can boost your own education by recruiting a volunteer who loves this technology! Many people are immersed in electronic communication and, like all "true believers," welcome the chance to help others get connected. Note that the type of person attracted to the volunteer position of "cyber deputy" or "Internet consultant" may be quite different in age, skills, or perhaps gender from your other applicants, already expanding the pool of talent your organization can tap. On the other hand, the Internet has become attractive to diverse populations, way beyond teenage boys! Seniors (driven by the realization that grandchildren will send e-mails) have come into cyberspace in droves. The gender gap is also rapidly closing. The "digital divide" is still real and the electronic world is not equally available to all income levels, but access to free computers in libraries, schools, and other sites is increasing quickly.

In 1996, I stressed:

First, if your organization does not yet have an e-mail address, get one. This piece of advice is going to look incredibly archaic to readers perhaps only a few years from now when having e-mail will be matter of fact. But today it still needs to be said. You cannot effectively use the wonders of cyberspace if people cannot reach you electronically.

Yes, this does indeed sound archaic in 2002! While the majority of North Americans today have an e-mail address at work and possibly access to e-mail at home (and it is fast expanding on other continents, too), it is not the case that volunteer program managers are using the power of e-mail in their recruitment outreach. Sure you can post messages online giving your telephone number. But the whole point of this new communications vehicle is that anyone can react instantly to a piece of information. So getting people online excited about joining your efforts without giving them an e-mail address is like opening an office without a road leading to your door.

If Not Your Home Page, Then Where?

If I surfed to your agency's Web site right now, would I immediately see—on the home page—that volunteers are involved in any aspect of your work? Would I find information on what volunteer positions are open and how to apply if I'm interested? Is there an online application form? Would I at least find the name, e-mail address, and telephone number of someone to contact about volunteering? If not—you have work to do!

Your organization's Web site is the most effective recruitment tool at your disposal. Yes, it's useful to register your volunteer opportunities with the online registries proliferating on the Web (more on those in a moment), but ultimately even those sources will direct prospective volunteers to your organization's own Web site. Will a visit to your site continue the recruitment process or become a dead end with no information?

Spend some time thinking about the design of a specific space for volunteer news and recruitment on the Web site. The beauty of cyberspace is that you can post absolutely everything you want to share with the public at no cost for paper printing, and those who enter your site can choose to access as much or as little information as they please. The person who looses interest in your material will exit; the prospective volunteer can read on.

When someone takes the time to click the button about volunteers on your home page, you are communicating with someone who wants more details. Provide them! Then the person will be well-informed and eager to express interest in volunteering. Use the multi-layered approach:

1. Home page: Mentions volunteer involvement and has a hotlink button for "more about volunteers."

2. Volunteer main page: An introduction to volunteers at your organization: what they do, who they are, how they are chosen. For each point, offer the choice to "learn more."

3 to ?. Further clicking might show:
- actual job descriptions for volunteer positions available now
- a wish list of skills or schedules needed
- photos of volunteers at work (showing diversity of age, race, gender)
- data on volunteer achievements
- personal testimonials from volunteers in certain assignments
- specific community service ideas for students
- specific ideas for groups or teams

Make sure that there are links to your volunteer information pages on every other page of the organization's Web site. Also take the step of registering your volunteer opportunities/information page with Web search engines and directories (your Webmaster or cyber deputy should be able to explain how).

Include the Web address on all printed materials (business cards, letterhead, brochures, newsletters, fax cover sheets, etc.). Remember to mention that there is volunteering information on your Web site in any newsletters, newspaper announcements, press releases, PSAs, etc. Why? Because most people in your target audiences who visit your Web site do so because of something they have read on paper or been told over the phone, not because they were surfing the Web.

For Membership Recruitment

If yours is an all-volunteer membership organization, then "how to join" will probably already be an option on the Web site. If not, it ought to be! But is the rest of the site's material presented in a way that is welcoming to newcomers? Or is it designed for current members who already know your goals, projects, and jargon? Consider posting pages directly addressed to non-members. Some topics might be:

- Why We Want You to Become a Member
  How getting more members will help your organization to reach its goals or have an impact through projects.

- Who We Want as Members
  Express your wishes about finding people with specific skills, or clarify that all ages, genders, family groups, etc. are all wanted (or not).

- What Are the Benefits of Joining?
  Share both the tangible (discounts) and intangible (friendship) perks.

- What Is Expected of New Members?
  If you want members to work as well as to "join," say so!

- The Membership Process
  Explain the steps (and timetable) from expressing interest to becoming a full-fledged member.

Immediate Response

It is crucial that you offer a way for interested people to respond immediately. Ideally, you'll have some sort of response mechanism right on the Web page, so that an interested person can click on "I'm interested, let's go to the next step..." and get a screen with a message form that is delivered electronically back to you. You can also offer an online application form.

Two important issues: timely response and updating your site. Cyberspace is a here-and-now environment. When someone sends an e-mail or a Web message, it is delivered to you instantly. So Netiquette demands a reasonably quick response or at least acknowledgment if not a complete answer. Check and deal with your e-mail often. Here is another great assignment for a volunteer who likes computers!

The humorous but ironic term for a Web site that never changes is a "cobWeb." Be sure you are not gathering virtual dust! The whole point of cyberspace is to go beyond the limits of the print media. Your Web page is not simply another newsletter. Once you print a newsletter on paper, it is permanent until replaced by the next edition.

Not so on the Web. You can—and should—update postings frequently to make it useful for people to enter your site often. There is a lot of competition on the Web today as new sites appear. What would make someone want to return to your site to see if any new volunteer opportunities are posted?

Recruitment of new volunteers is not the only reason to design pages on your Web site. Think about the possibilities for recognition! For example, post photographs of volunteer activities immediately after they occur (or during—if you have a digital camera). Not only does this make those individual volunteers feel appreciated right away (why wait until the banquet months later?), but it reinforces the idea of volunteers as active, year-round contributors for any site visitor, including paid staff, donors, clients, and—yes—prospective volunteers. This changing kaleidoscope of photos also enlivens the site, avoiding stagnant pages.

Resistance from the Webmaster

It's at this point that some readers will be thinking that the Red Sea will part again before their agency's Webmaster or MIS staff will give this much Web space—and programming time—to volunteer involvement. So, as with many other tasks of volunteer program management, you may have to do some in-house education.

First, be prepared with a detailed list of the pages and content you are requesting. Don't expect the Web designer to know what to say or how to recruit. Present your material on a disk or as an e-mail attachment. If you arrive with the content in hand, then the work you require from the Webmaster is mainly page design and posting. Don't walk away! Stay involved in choosing illustrative material, colors, etc. This is what you would do with a printer and the same principle applies to Web work.

Second, if you feel that you are being put lowest on the totem pole for work priority, offer to recruit a volunteer to design the pages for you. The Web master will legitimately want to do the actual posting (making the pages show up online) and have approval of anything that goes on the Web site. But that doesn't mean someone else can't program the text and pictures into HTML or other Web formats. Another great job for a volunteer cyber deputy.

You may have to take this issue all the way up to your top executive. Web masters do not set priorities for the organization. They take their orders from agency decision makers. You need to make your case to administration that time spent now on building the volunteer area on the Web site is important for the long run. If the site already asks for donations of money, note that "people raising" and "fund raising" go together.

Finally, spend some time online to find good examples of Web sites that present volunteer involvement in a way you like. This not only gives you "ammunition" against resistance, but also models to follow.

If all else fails and you are unable to get online through your organization, obtain permission to post a Web site specifically for the volunteer program. This is not hard, nor very expensive, to do. And there are sites online that will host a nonprofit organization's Web pages for free.

Other Online Recruitment Opportunities

Recruiting on the Internet has amazing potential to attract endless numbers and types of applicants, but electronic outreach can be time-consuming, both to post opportunities and to keep the information updated and current. This is why you should start by recruiting volunteers who are intrigued by searching the Web for sites that list volunteer opportunities or targeted places to post recruitment messages. Here are some of the ways the Internet and especially the World Wide Web can become recruitment tools for you.

Research

Your ability to locate vast amounts of information electronically is limited only by your time and your creativity. Learn about the work of other organizations that might become sources of volunteers or collaborative partners, from businesses to nonprofit agencies, to all-volunteer service clubs—whether you contact them online or off-line. Discover the ways other volunteers are doing their work that might be applied to your situation. Locate other people who share your interests or concerns, or who are willing to answer your questions (via e-mail, usually) on any subject. Find interesting tidbits to enliven your newsletter. Searching for information online is most fruitful if you can formulate specific questions to answer, rather than going on a "fishing expedition" without a goal.

Online Volunteer Opportunity Registries

New Web sites are springing up with the goal of assisting the nonprofit community in general and volunteering in particular. We have not even begun to imagine the possibilities. They all share several things in common right now. They are free, and you can post and update your entries at will. They allow prospective volunteers to search for opportunities by zip/postal code and by interest. They are growing in popularity as people become aware of the accessibility of this sort of information online.

Unfortunately, they also share another characteristic: most of the postings are too general and many are out of date. Remember that the Web allows you to be as specific as necessary. Better to post ten detailed position descriptions that really help people to self-screen their interest than to post one "Hometown Agency Needs Help" ad that gives no real information at all. And return to the site and delete assignments no longer available or update those that are.

As of this book's third edition, the most popular online registry in the United States is VolunteerMatch: www.volunteermatch.org. It's a great place to start testing online directories, especially as it is the database used by other philanthropy Web sites such as Network For Good (www.networkforgood.org). Registries have developed in many other countries, too, including Canada (www.voe-reb.org/welcome.jhtml), the United Kingdom (www.thesite.org/do-it/), Australia (www.govolunteer.com.au/), and also in non-English speaking countries. Some sites encourage international postings, recruiting volunteers from one country to help organizations anywhere in the world. Look at Action Without Borders (www.idealist.org) as one example. For the most current list of all such sites, go to the Energize, Inc. Web site page: www.energizeinc.com/prof/volop.html

The commercial online services, such as America Online and CompuServe, have created special interest areas devoted exclusively to community involvement and nonprofit organizations. Recruit links to each of the various commercial services by asking volunteers and employees who subscribe to any online service at home to search for community involvement sites and describe these to you. Give them disks with your recruitment messages and e-mail address and ask that they post these for you.

As time goes on, more people will grow accustomed to turning to the Internet for information about volunteering and therefore it is smart to make use of any and all online registries. Of course, no national site can ever hope to contain all the volunteer opportunities available in a country—the list is far larger than any paid job bank might be and no one expects to find all employment openings in one place. For this reason, a growing number of Volunteer Centers are also posting their databases of local volunteer opportunities online. Various community Web sites also welcome information about volunteering alongside other public notices about events, recreation, and other social activities occurring in a region. If you are seeking volunteers only for one location, it may be more fruitful to post openings on a local site rather than on a national database, although anecdotal reports from colleagues claim that prospects do respond to such postings. Certainly, if you need volunteers at a number of locations, or if someone can help you without having to come on site, the national registries provide one more way to spread the word.

Online Discussion Groups

People with mutual interests can communicate amazingly quickly and cheaply in cyberspace. Through "listservs" and similar vehicles, a host or sponsor group can maintain a literally limitless number of names and e-mail addresses and send the same messages simultaneously (and almost instantly) to everyone—anywhere on the globe. When you "subscribe" to an online discussion or electronic publication, your e-mailbox receives all the messages sent that day. If you choose to reply to one of the messages, your response will similarly be sent to everyone on the list. There is usually no charge for being on the subscriber list and you can "unsubscribe" just as quickly.

"Newsgroups" or "message boards" operate very much like online discussion forums, but are not "delivered" directly to your e-mailbox. They are an electronic form of the old-fashioned thumbtack bulletin board on which members interact by posting queries and replies. You read through these at a specific Web site or through your Internet browser.

Listservs and newsgroups span a mind-boggling array of subjects and therefore are wonderful for finding the specific skills and interests that match your volunteer position openings. The point for a recruiter is that such groups gather like-minded individuals who might be candidates as volunteers. It is target marketing heaven! Looking for people who can teach bicycle safety to your teens? Find a bicyclist newsgroup. Want to find an architect with experience in designing tree houses? Dip into an architecture or an outdoor recreation listserv.

It's always a good idea to spend some time "listening in" (also called "lurking") before joining in the virtual conversation. That way you will learn about the culture and type of messages each group attracts. Some lists reject postings that read like an advertisement. But if you explain who (and where) you are and why you are using this format to locate someone with these particular skills, you should not have a problem posting your message. If in doubt, take the trouble to introduce yourself courteously to the group hosts first and ask how best to access their group.

Remember that board users can be located anywhere, so add your city to the subject line of your posting, so that when someone is browsing the board, it is easy to open or pass by the message headed:

"Apply your editing skills in Baltimore!"
"Toronto youth seek soccer coach"

A good place to look for appropriate newsgroups and listservs is via these Web sites:

http://www.liszt.com
http://www.tile.net
http://groups.google.com

E-mail Newsbriefs and Communiqués

Even without a Web site, you can generate electronic communication and send it to a long list of interested people at no printing or postage cost at all. Keep an "address book" of e-mail addresses and develop regular news updates to keep your organization on people's minds. Remember that the instant nature of cyberspace allows you to advertise a volunteer assignment the same day it becomes open. Whenever you send out a press release to the traditional media, make an electronic copy and e-mail it out, too.

This type of low-cost, immediate communication makes it possible for the first time for a national headquarters to share information with and request action from members at all levels of the organization. Further, when combined with an available message board, members can be encouraged to deal directly with each other to exchange views, share suggestions, and find support. This removes the middle layer of interaction—no longer do people have to go through a national or state office to identify and reach their colleagues.

Intranets

Many larger corporations and national organizations maintain "intranets." So do colleges and universities. These are internal communication systems that operate just as regular e-mail but only within that setting. Access is denied to anyone not in the company, organization, or school. However, such in-house systems often have electronic newsletters and other regular announcements of activities of interest to employees or members. See if you can contact the person responsible for running the intranet and offer an electronic recruitment message. This is very similar to working with the editor of a printed in-house newsletter.

Some intranets allow members to post messages themselves. In that case, ask volunteers who work in companies with this type of system or who are students at a university to advertise volunteer opportunities for you. This has the added bonus of serving as an endorsement of the organization from a work/study colleague already involved as a volunteer.

Cross-Linking

Many supporters of your organization will have Web sites of their own, both for their businesses and for personal use. Possibilities include donors, vendors, volunteers, employees—even clients. Ask them if they would like to show their support by publicly linking to your site. This is an easy and cost-free way for them to help you and for you to increase your outreach to whole new circles of people.

Design an electronic "button" or "banner" with your logo and a brief message that can easily be posted and hotlinked. Some simple ideas are:

I am a proud volunteer at XYZ Agency. To learn more, click here.

See why I support XYZ Agency. Click here.

You can even make this a part of volunteer recognition. Design the button to look like an award or medal, saying:

XYZ Agency applauds _____ for her excellent volunteer service this year. Learn more.

Volunteer Achievement Award to _____ for service to XYZ Agency. Want to join him? Click here.

Of course it should be any volunteers' choice as to whether or not to post this, but you at least are giving them the means to make their service visible.

Another idea is to approach for-profit businesses to post information about your organization on their Web sites as a "public service" or a donation of space. Because of "hot link" technology, this brief mention can allow the intrigued user to click instantly to your Web pages to learn more.

Similarly, cooperating nonprofits can cross-link their organizations on all their Web sites. This can be an effective public outreach tool for special events or in times of emergency. For example, after the terrorist attack on New York City on September 11, 2001, several Web sites immediately responded with information from many sources on how concerned citizens could help. These collective postings were of benefit to people in many other locations as well as to New Yorkers.

Be Ready to Respond

Asking for volunteers but not having a method to immediately place them into your volunteer program is like advertising a product you don't really have, and it can cause hard feelings about your agency on the part of potential supporters. If your organization cannot or does not answer e-mail within 48 hours of receipt, don't include your e-mail address as a way for potential volunteers to contact you. Instead, in your online announcements, direct volunteers to telephone you. Make sure those who answer your agency's phone know you are posting information to the Internet, in case there is an increase in phone calls regarding volun-

teer opportunities or in people referring to "that e-mail you posted."

When providing volunteer information online, whether in the form of an announcement or a Web page, remember to include your organization's name, postal address, phone number, and e-mail address.

Broader Application of Cyberspace

This book is focused on volunteer recruitment, but cyberspace has implications for other aspects of volunteer program management as well. In fact we have coined a whole new term, "virtual volunteering," to refer to ways that people (the volunteers are real) can offer help via their computers (the activity is virtual). For example, there are many ways that technical assistance can be given through e-mail and downloaded files, from the sharing of legal or real estate expertise, to editing of press releases, to explanations of how a colleague handled a similar problem. Virtual volunteering can also involve "friendly visiting" by computer, self-help support groups online, or playing computer games with hospital-bound youngsters. Much more information about online service can be found at www.serviceleader.org/vv and through *The Virtual Volunteering Guidebook* (Ellis & Cravens, 2000), available for free download at: www.energizeinc.com/art/elecbooks.html

Fundraising by electronic means is tantalizing many with its possibilities. The potential of "distance learning," in which trainees log online for a "class" taught by an instructor who can be miles away is easy to imagine. Think about the applications to providing orientation and training to off-site volunteers.

For the record, recognize that almost all the transactions in cyberspace are a form of mutual assistance by people who do their keyboarding in their leisure time: volunteers! Many online hosts and Web site managers, and millions of people posting information and responding to e-mail do all this because they really like it and also like serving others. Certainly commercial interests have gotten into the act, but right now this wild West, new frontier of communication is a prime example of volunteers as pioneers. So someone recruiting should feel right at home!

References

The following books and articles are mentioned in the text. Those books with an asterisk (*) are available from Energize, Inc., 5450 Wissahickon Avenue, Philadelphia, PA 19144, 1-800-395-9800 or from our Online Bookstore at http://www.energizeinc.com/ bkstore.html.

Acker, Phyllis. "The Nominating Committee: Essential to the Organization." *The Journal of Volunteer Administration*, II, 2 (Winter 1983-84), pp. 29-33.

Brown, Kathleen M. "'Share the Heart': An Innovative Way to Involve Church Members in the Community." *Voluntary Action Leadership* (Summer *1985*), p. 19.

Dodson, Dorian. *How to Recruit Great Board Members*. Santa Fe, NM: Adolfo Street Publications, 1993.

Ellis, Susan J. *From the Top Down: The Executive Role in Volunteer Program Success*. Philadelphia: Energize, 1986. Revised edition, 1996.*

Ellis, Susan J. *Volunteer Centers: Gearing Up for the 1990s*. Alexandria, VA: United Way of America, 1989. As of 2001, only available electronically at http://www.energizeinc.com/art/elecbooks.html

Ellis, Susan J. and Katherine H. Noyes. *By the People: A History of Americans as Volunteers*, revised edition. San Francisco: Jossey-Bass Publishers, 1990. Third edition to be published by Energize, Inc. in 2002.

Fischer, Lucy Rose and Kay Banister Schaffer. *Older Volunteers: A Guide to Research and Practice*. Newbury Park, CA: Sage Publications, 1993.

Macduff, Nancy. *Episodic Volunteering: Building the Short-term Volunteer Program*. Walla Walla, WA: MBA Publishing, 1991.

Martin, Mike W. *Virtuous Giving: Philanthropy, Voluntary Service and Caring*. Bloomington: Indiana University Press, 1994.

Scheier, Ivan H. *Building Staff-Volunteer Relations*. Philadelphia: Energize, 1993. *

Scheier, Ivan H. *When Everyone's a Volunteer: The Effective Functioning of All-Volunteer Groups*. Philadelphia: Energize, 1992. *

Schindler-Rainman, Eva. *Transitioning: Strategies for the Volunteer World*. Vancouver, BC: Voluntary Action Resource Centre, 1981.

Sutton, Charyn D. *Pass It On: Outreach to Minority Communities*. Philadelphia: Big Brothers/Big Sisters of America, 1992.

Tremper, Charles and Gwynne Kostin. *No Surprises: Controlling Risks in Volunteer Programs.* Washington, DC: Nonprofit Risk Management Center, 1993. New edition, 2002. *

Tufts, Suzanne, Charles Tremper, Anna Seidman, and Jeffrey Kahn. *Legal Barriers to Volunteer Service.* Washington, DC: Nonprofit Risk Management Center, 1994.

Vineyard, Sue and Steve McCurley (eds.). *Managing Volunteer Diversity: A Rainbow of Opportunities.* Downers Grove, IL: Heritage Arts Publishing, 1992.

Virginia Office of Volunteerism. "The Americans with Disabilities Act: Information and Implications for Volunteer Program Administrators." Richmond, VA: 1992.

Young, Christine L., Pamela J. Larson, and Donald Goughler. "Organizations as Volunteers for the Rural Frail Elderly," The *Journal of Volunteer Administration*, II, 1 (Fall 1983), pp. 33-44.

Over the years, there have been many excellent articles published on many aspects of volunteer recruitment. See if your local Volunteer Center or a colleague who is a long-time director of volunteers has back issues of *The Journal of Volunteer Administration* or *Volunteer Leadership* (in the United States) or whatever similar publication is available in your country. For the newest books that include a section on recruitment, including finding volunteers for special settings, start by looking at the Energize Online Bookstore at http://www.energizeinc.com/ bkstore.html.

Index